The Civil Rights Struggle for Freedom and Equality in America

Naoual Kamal
Karima Bouziane

The Civil Rights Struggle for Freedom and Equality in America

Amiri Baraka's Dutchman and The Slave

LAP LAMBERT Academic Publishing

Impressum / Imprint

Bibliografische Information der Deutschen Nationalbibliothek: Die Deutsche Nationalbibliothek verzeichnet diese Publikation in der Deutschen Nationalbibliografie; detaillierte bibliografische Daten sind im Internet über http://dnb.d-nb.de abrufbar.

Alle in diesem Buch genannten Marken und Produktnamen unterliegen warenzeichen-, marken- oder patentrechtlichem Schutz bzw. sind Warenzeichen oder eingetragene Warenzeichen der jeweiligen Inhaber. Die Wiedergabe von Marken, Produktnamen, Gebrauchsnamen, Handelsnamen, Warenbezeichnungen u.s.w. in diesem Werk berechtigt auch ohne besondere Kennzeichnung nicht zu der Annahme, dass solche Namen im Sinne der Warenzeichen- und Markenschutzgesetzgebung als frei zu betrachten wären und daher von jedermann benutzt werden dürften.

Bibliographic information published by the Deutsche Nationalbibliothek: The Deutsche Nationalbibliothek lists this publication in the Deutsche Nationalbibliografie; detailed bibliographic data are available in the Internet at http://dnb.d-nb.de.

Any brand names and product names mentioned in this book are subject to trademark, brand or patent protection and are trademarks or registered trademarks of their respective holders. The use of brand names, product names, common names, trade names, product descriptions etc. even without a particular marking in this work is in no way to be construed to mean that such names may be regarded as unrestricted in respect of trademark and brand protection legislation and could thus be used by anyone.

Coverbild / Cover image: www.ingimage.com

Verlag / Publisher:
LAP LAMBERT Academic Publishing
ist ein Imprint der / is a trademark of
OmniScriptum GmbH & Co. KG
Heinrich-Böcking-Str. 6-8, 66121 Saarbrücken, Deutschland / Germany
Email: info@lap-publishing.com

Herstellung: siehe letzte Seite /
Printed at: see last page
ISBN: 978-3-659-77764-6

Zugl. / Approved by: University of Mainz, Germany, Diss., 2015

Acknowledgment

Our thanks and gratitude goes to Professor Sabina Matter-Seibel, from university of Mainz Germany, for proofreading this work, for her support, guidance and constructive criticism.

Table of Contents

1 Introduction

The civil rights movement, one of the fundamental reform impulses of the last century, attempted to eliminate racial segregation, securing greater social and political equality for black Americans in The United States. Indeed, black Americans were excluded from real equality, included mainly in their voting rights as well as the rigid anti-black laws known as Jim Crow. This series of laws touched every aspect of everyday life. It mandated, for instance, the segregation of public schools, public places and public transportation. In other words, the southern states rewrote their constitutions so as to separate blacks and whites from birth to burial (Dierenfield 10).

This book will deal with the civil rights struggle for freedom and equality in the 1950s and the 1960s in America. Besides, a study of *Dutchman* and *The Slave*, two famous plays of the black activist LeRoi Jones or Amiri Baraka will constitute the basis of this paper.

To begin with, seminal victories of the civil rights movement during the 1950s will be discussed in the first part of the book. In fact, the Brown v. Board of Education (1954) presented a crucial Supreme Court decision that invalidated "separate-but-equal" public schools, offering a great triumph for the NAACP´s members in fighting for school integration. A separate chapter will deal with the Montgomery, Alabama Bus Boycott of 1955-1956, stating the role of Rosa Parks in changing the law in America. In the next chapter, the Little Rock Crisis, in which nine African American students known as the "Little Rock Nine" were escorted inside Little Rock Central High School by troops of the 101st Airborne Division of The United States Army, will be discussed.

The second part of this book will be dedicated to the most influential African American leaders of the twentieth century. In essence, Martin Luther King, Jr. and Malcolm X are highly controversial African American leaders in life and in point of view about justice and racial discrimination. They shared, however, the goal for which they fought. While King employed the tactics of civil protest to end racial segregation admiring support from black and white Americans, Malcolm X rejected the strategy of nonviolence. But he changed his thinking after his split with the Nation of Islam.

In the third part, the career of Amiri Baraka as author and black politician will be analyzed. The first chapter will deal with the former LeRoi Jones who spent a usual childhood. His parents encouraged him to educate and to do social interaction. At Howard University, Jones began to form his opinions about the black middle class which he found was most harmful to black culture in general. After graduating from Howard, Jones entered the Air Force, where he completely understood the pain of racism which addresses the image of the blacks. After publishing his first collection of poems, *Preface to a Twenty Volume Suicide Note*, which were clearly marked by hopelessness and disillusionment, he made a trip to Cuba. Later on, Jones started to establish a black movement in Greenwich Village. Baraka´s life as a political activist will be portrayed in the second chapter. His anger was clearly noticed through his political views and activities. As a leader of the Revolutionary Theatre, he showed the hostility of the whites towards the blacks.

This book will devote the last part to the analysis of Jones´ two plays *Dutchman* and *The Slave*. The first chapter will introduce *Dutchman* as a powerful voice to the American theatre. Furthermore, the main themes in the play as well as the notion of Black man as a victim will be examined in two chapters. In the next chapter Metaphorical Representations for America and the Oppressed will be studied offering the viewer seemingly infinite number of truths. Jones depicts also identity confusion of the middle-class Black Clay, stating that the survival of the Black man in America requires keeping his true identity hidden. Admitting that *Dutchman* is rooted in symbolism, a chapter will discuss the significance of the main symbols used in the play. In addition, the gender roles of the characters as well as the language used in the play will be examined in the next two chapters. The shocking language in *Dutchman* governs, in fact, the characters and their actions.

Jones´ second play *The Slave* will be analyzed through the discussion of its main themes. The playwright continues exploring his racial hatred and black revolution. Two chapters will be dedicated to two paradoxical features of the central character Walker Vessels. Being a revolutionary leader of the blacks and a victim of his philosophy can merely indicate Walker´s ambiguity. As a writer of the Black Arts Movement, Baraka expresses his rage and violence through the language and the narrative devices he employed in The Slave. Moreover, the last part of this book will devote a chapter to a comparison between the two boldly radical plays *Dutchman* and *The Slave*. Both of the plays offer several striking parallels and reversals, but they share the issue of racial revolution.

2 The fight for Civil Rights in America during the 1950s

Reading the American History reveals the horrible conditions under which African Americans lived, and how they fought for equal rights for all citizens in America.

About a little more than one tenth of all United States citizens are descended from people brought across the Atlantic from Africa as slaves. The history of blacks in North America began in August 1619, when a Dutch warship, that sailed up the James River to the young English colony of Jamestown, Virginia, captured a Spanish ship in the Caribbean Sea carrying black men and women to Spanish colonies in South America (Virginia's First Africans).

The Jamestown colonists needed at that time workers to build houses and plant crops. Large plantations brought of course harsh working conditions. Gradually, the slave trade boomed during the 18th century and it was usual for farmers to own one or two slaves.

So, slavery existed in practically all the North American colonies. As the American colonists fought at the end of the 18th century for independence from Britain, a call for self-determination, equality and recognition of the natural rights of man was

3

arisen. Many advocates of American freedom criticized slavery and campaigned for dignity for all Blacks. In fact, Blacks encountered in the early years of the 20th century discrimination in jobs and public places. At that time, it would have to take action to end segregation. The 1950s brought really the beginning of major change.

2.1 Brown v. Board of Education, 1954

Although the Civil War did bring an official end to slavery in the United States, it did not manage to erase the huge gap between blacks and whites. In fact, African Americans were often treated differently than whites in many parts of the country. Blacks and whites, for example, dined at separate restaurants, bathed in separate swimming pools, and attended separate schools. These regulations came to be known as Jim Crow laws that enforced segregation of the races and limited, therefore, the rights of the blacks.

In 1896, the Supreme Court upheld the precedent of "separate but equal" established by *Plessy v. Ferguson*. The legislation of two separate societies was, therefore, permitted as long as the two were equal. However, African Americans felt that these laws were unjust. They began to fight for the abolition of racially discriminatory laws. One such law required blacks and whites to attend separate schools. In essence, there was no equality in educational system regarding to qualifications and salaries of teachers as well as schools buildings.

Unlike good conditions in white schools, black students were crowded together in shanties without electricity, blackboards, or desks. They walked also long distances to a school of blacks. It was time to demand an end to Jim Crew Laws and all forms of racial inequality. One particular organization that fought for racial equality of all persons was the National Association for the Advancement of Colored People (NAACP), founded on February 12, 1909 by a diverse group composed of W.E.B Du Bois, Ida Wells- Barnett, Mary White Ovington, and others. Their mission was to fight racial and social injustice, primarily through legal action.

4

The NAACP´s Legal department, beginning in the 1930, was headed by Charles Hamilton and Thurgood Marshall, who learned the law at Howard University in Washington, DC, the capstone of black education. Marshall knew, in essence, how racism stymied black ambitions because he was denied admission to the University of Maryland. He often asked black youngsters what they wanted to do when they grew up. Their ambitions were to become butlers, postmen, or maids. Dierenfield pointed out: „Marshall realized that these children were already defeated psychologically"(Dierenfield 22).

Marshall argued that black children sent to black segregated schools felt inferior even though they possessed the same ability as whites, which made learning nearly impossible. Marshall and the NAACP´s members began challenging the Supreme Court to strike down school segregation laws. They were convinced that if they sued a state to make its schools for black children equal to those for whites, then they could challenge segregation itself. However, the road to Brown v. Board of Education, 1954, what contributed mightily to the civil rights movement, was not easy. The NAACP had to launch a series of suits attacking segregation in education and seeking full and fair equality in schools.

Beginning in 1936, the NAACP Legal Defense and Education Fund decided to take on the case of Lloyd Gaines, an African American student who had been refused admission to the University of Missouri Law School. The state of Missouri offered to pay his expenses for law school outside the state since it did not have any all- black school in Missouri at this time. Gaines rejected this offer and cited that it violated his Fourteenth Amendment right. With the help of the NAACP Legal Defense and Education Fund, Gaines decided to sue the state so as to attend the University of Missouri ´s law school. By 1938, the case of Gaines reached the U.S Supreme Court.

Charles Hamilton Houston argued that Missouri was obliged to either build a law school for blacks equal to that of whites or admit Gaines to the University of Missouri. The Supreme Court decided in favor of Lloyd Gaines. The six member majority stated that since a black law school did not exist in the state of Missouri, it could not send Gaines to another state. "The Gaines decision breached the walls of segregation. It means that every state now either had to build a separate graduate school for blacks or integrate" (Wormser). In response to the Gaines decision, state officials in Missouri opened a law school at the all black Lincoln University.

Ten years later, the United States Supreme Court ruled in Sipiuel v. Board of Regents of University of Oklahoma, that the state of Oklahoma must provide instruction for blacks equal to that of whites. Ada Lois Sipuel Fisher, the daughter of an African American minister, applied in 1946 at the University of Oklahoma law school so as to challenge the state´s segregation laws and to become a lawyer. Fisher was disappointed as she was denied admission to the University solely because of her race; she appealed to the U.S. Supreme Court. Supported by the civil right attorney Thurgood Marshall, who cited Missouri Gaines case, the U.S. Supreme Court agreed to hear Sipuel´s case. Marshall argued that Oklahoma´s law school must open its doors to Sipuel, and the doctrine of "separate but equal" should be abandoned (NAACP & the Ada Sipuel Case).

On June 18, 1949 Sipuel was admitted to the University of Oklahoma law school, and she became the first African American woman who attended an all-white law school in the South. Oklahoma decided later to open a new law school for African Americans. The NAACP continued nonetheless its fight against segregation in education. Working in collaboration with Marshall, the South Carolina civil rights worker, Joseph Armstrong De Laine and Modejska Monteith Simkins, sought twenty local residents in Clarendon Country to sign a petition for educational equality. More particularly, the petioners cited compelling evidence that show a huge inequality in the public schools in Clarendon Country: "During the school year 1949-50, Clarendon Country spent $149 per white child in the public schools, as opposed to $43 for each black child. The total value of the sixty-one black schools, attended by 6531 students, was listed officially as $194 575; the value of the twelve white schools, accommodating 2375 students, was placed at $673 850" (Patterson 25).

6

In fact, black people in Clarendon Country represented 70 percent of population, which reveals that racial discrimination was glaring. None of black students, for instance, had bus transportation. They were forced to walk for miles to get to school. So, to provide buses for black children was mainly the request of the black parents in Clarendon Country. They asked the local school superintendent, R.M. Elliott to provide a bus for their children. Elliott refused, arguing that black citizens did not pay enough taxes to support a bus (Dierenfield 23). In 1949, the petition was signed by more than 100 Clarenden residents. The first two names on the list were Harry Briggs, a service station attendant, and his wife, Eliza Briggs, who worked as a maid. Both of them were fired and most of the petitioners paid a price for their courage. They were, in essence, economically punished for their role in the case. They were, for example, denied credit, told to pay up debts at once or to be foreclosed. DeLaine lost also his job as principal of Silver Grade School and he received threatening letters. He had to flee the state when his home was burned down (23).

The Briggs case reached finally in late May 1951 federal district court in Charleston where the three judge federal panel Walter Warring, George Bell Timmerman and John Parker heard the case. Preparing the process, attorney Robert Carter used the social science testimony to show how segregation retards the mental and educational development of black school children, including evidence from psychologists Kenneth Clark and his wife Mamie Clark´s controversial „Doll Study". Clarks designed, during the 1940s, a test to study the psychological effects of segregation on black children. The doll experiment involved a child being presented with two dolls. Both of them were totally identical except for the skin and hair color. The child chose to play with the white doll with yellow hair, and considered it the nice one. This test showed that all children in the study, who were attending segregated schools, preferred white dolls over black ones (Brown at 60: The Doll Test). Showing a preference for the white doll is ,in fact, a clear sign of black self-hate." One black child smiled when asked whom the black doll resembled: "...that´s a nigger. I´m a nigger" (Dierenfield 23).

Black children have negative views about their skin, to the point of making them hate themselves. They judged the white skin as superior to the black one. Clark's findings attracted the attention of the NAACP members, who believed that it could be effectively used in court to show how segregation harmed black school children, and damaged their personality development. Therefore, Clark became the Legal Defense Fund's principal expert witness. The court, however, ruled against Briggs and the other parents from Clarendon Country. It argued that the Country must only make facilities equal.

Although the NAACP's attorneys were disappointed by the court's decision, they did not give up, encouraged by their victory in Sweatt v. Painter and Mc Laurin v. Oklahoma State Regents' cases in 1950. The first case began in 1946 when Herman Sweatt, an African American student, applied to the University of Texas White Law School that rejected his application for the reason that Texas's constitution prohibited integrated education. So, the state had to build a law school for black students, which had been established in a downtown basement (Patterson 16). Sweatt was not satisfied. He employed the services of the NAACP and sued to be admitted to the University's white law school. This case, presented by W.J. Durham and Thurgood Marshall, reached the U.S. Supreme Court. The attorneys argued that University of Texas Law School's educational level was far superior in its offerings and resources to the separate Black law school.

More particularly, they cited some facts supporting the differences between white and black facilities in the University of Texas Law School:

> "The University of Texas Law School had 16 full-time and 3 part-time professors, while the black law school had 5 full-time professors. The University of Texas Law School had 850 students and a law library of 65,000 volumes, while the black law school had 23 students and a library of 16,500 volumes"(Sweatt v. Painter).

The Supreme Court decided in favor of Sweatt, pointing out that the law school of black students could not be equal to the University of Texas Law School.

Sweatt's case together with McLaurin v. Oklahoma State Regents, which was decided the same day, indicated that segregated schools failed to provide equal education. The University of Oklahoma admitted, in fact, in 1949 the African American student, George McLaurin, to pursue a Doctor of Education degree. However, it provided him separate facilities. It required him, for instance, to sit apart from the rest of the class, to use a designated desk in the library and to eat at a separate table in the campus cafeteria, etc (Patterson 17).

McLaurin, stating that these arrangements were dehumanizing and resulting in opposite effects on his academic studies, sued to require the University of Oklahoma to remove the segregated actions. The NAACP´ s team took the case to the U.S. Supreme Court, which agreed that these restrictions were unconstitutional. It ordered the University to end such actions that inhibit McLaurin´ s ability to study.

Thus, Marshall and his legal team Robert Carter, Jack Greenberg, George Hayes, James Nabrit, Jr., and Spottswood Robinson pursued the strategy that had led to the triumphs of Sweatt and McLaurin to challenge segregation in the five suits known collectively as Brown v. Board of Education. These lawsuits were Brown v. Board of Education of Topeka, Briggs v. Elliott, Davis v. Board of Education of Prince Edward County, Boiling v. Sharpe, and Gebhart v. Ethel. Although the facts of each case were different, they exposed the vast discrepancies between white and black schools.

In Topeka, Kansas, Oliver Brown, an African American assistant pastor at the church, sued to end the segregated school system. His seven-year-old daughter Linda Brown had to cross a dangerous railroad yard to her school bus that carried her a mile away to the segregated black school, while the white Summer Elementary School was seven blocks from her house. Other black parents joined Brown and complained. The board chairman replied gruffly: " We ain´t got money to buy a bus for your nigger children."(Dierenfield 23)

So, Brown and twelve other plaintiffs went to the NAACP´s team and asked for help. The local NAACP filed suit in federal district court on February 28, 1951. This action did not really arouse reactions until June, 1952 when the Supreme Court heard the Brown case and combined it with Briggs. Relying on the testimony of sociologist Kenneth Clark and other data, the NAACP´ s attorneys argued that segregated school system caused damage to black children, and made them feel inferior to whites. The judges of the Supreme Court acknowledged on the one hand, that segregation of white and black children in public schools gave the colored children a feeling of inferiority, which affected their motivation to learn. On the other hand, the judges did not dare to reverse the „separate but equal" doctrine in Plessy (Brown v. Board of Education). Failed to reach a decision, the Supreme Court scheduled Brown and Briggs cases to be heard in December, and it combined them with other three school segregation cases in Virginia, the District of Columbia and Delaware.

The petitioners of Davis v. Board of Education of Prince Edward and Boiling v. Sharpe´s cases were African Americans students, who yearned for equal opportunities in black schools. In April 1951, the students, led by 16 year-old Barbara Johns, went on strike and demanded better facilities in their school. The strike lasted ten days until the NAACP attorney, Oliver Hill, met the striking students and promised them to file suit in the federal district court in Richmond (Davis v. School Board of Prince Edward County (Virginia). The Virginia case was filed as Dorothy E. Davis v. County School Board of Prince Edward County since the first student listed was the ninth grade girl, Dorothy Davis.

Boiling v. Sharpe case began as the eleven African American junior high school youths were refused admission to the new Sousa High School for white student, which provided better facilities for students. On September 11, 1950 Garduer Bishop, a minister and a community leader, encouraged the parents of the black children to take action in order to request equal opportunities for their children. Led by James

10

Narbit, Howard University professor of law, the case of Boiling v. Sharpe was filed in 1951 in U.S. District Court, in Washington, DC and it was named for Spottswood Thomas Boiling, one of the children who denied admission to Sousa High School solely because of his race (Patterson 30).

Contrary to the previous cases of Brown v. Board of Education, Gebhart v. Belton´s case involved two separate actions but with identical issues. The first case was developed in the suburb of Claymont, where the African American students could not attend the well- maintained school in Claymont. They were forced, by law, to attend the segregated Howard High School located in an undesirable section of Willmington. So, the parents of eight African American students asked state education officials to admit their children to the local Claymont School. They were, however, denied.

The other case took place in the rural community of Hockessin, where the black student, Shirley Barbara had to walk every day to the old one-room schoolhouse designated for African American children. Her mother, Sarah Bulah, filed suit on behalf of her daughter and other plaintiffs against the state Board of Education of the state of Delaware for racial equality (qtd. in Patterson, *Brown v. Board of Education*). The Belton and Bulah cases were both filed in the Delaware Court by the NAACP´s lawyer Louis Redding.

As I mentioned before, all these five cases were combined by the Supreme Court into a single case known as Brown v. Board of Education. After contentious meetings of the justices of the Supreme Court, the case was reheard in December 1953, and the Court had a new Chief Justice, the California governor, Earl Warren, with whom the most visible Supreme Court decision in American History would be declared. On May 17, 1954 the Court overturned *Plessy v. Ferguson*, and declared unanimously racial segregation in public schools unconstitutional. Chief Justice Earl Warren concluded the decision of the Court: "... We conclude that in the field of public education the doctrine of ´separate- but-equal´ has no place. Separate educational facilities are inherently unequal." (Patterson 67)

In essence, the Brown v. Board of Education decision presented a great triumph for the NAACP´s members in fighting, for more than forty years, against racial educational inequality. This decision, however, could not abolish discrimination in other public areas in the South of the United States.

2.2 Rosa Parks and the Montgomery Bus Boycott, 1955-1956

For many years, Jim Crow laws had kept African Americans and whites apart. Blacks and whites attended separate schools, dined at separate restaurants, bathed in separate swimming pools, and drank from separate water fountains. Jim Crow laws existed mainly in the South of the United States. In Montgomery, for instance, only white people could ride in the front of the bus, while African Americans had to sit in the back of it, where the "colored" section reserved for them. Moreover, black riders were required to enter from the rear of the bus and to move or stand when there were no white-only seats left in the bus.

Montgomery´s black citizens were tired of this social injustice, and they complained that these treatments they received every day of their life were unfair. Black activists began, in fact, to build a case so as to challenge state bus segregation laws in the South when Claudette Colvin, a 15-year-old student and an active member in the NAACP Youth Council, was arrested on March 2, 1955. The policeman kicked her and knocked her school books away just because she refused to give her seat in the bus to a white passenger (Dierenfield 44). With the goal of challenging segregation on the city´ s public buses in Montgomery, Edgar Daniel Nixon, president of the local chapter of the NAACP, thought he had found the right person. Colvin was unfortunately teenager and her out-of-wedlock pregnancy might have caused problems.

Nine months later, an African American woman, named Rosa Parks, was arrested for refusing, under the Jim Crow law, to surrender her bus seat in the colored section to a white passenger (45). Parks seemed to be a good candidate to test the segregation laws in court. She was a seamstress by profession, was happily married, and she was active in the Civil Rights Movement by serving as secretary of the NAACP. It was truly a perfect combination to get the society´s attention. Rosa Parks refused Jim Crow law when she would not move to the back of the bus. Her courageous act reflected, in fact, how she was tired of all kinds of racial injustice she and other African Americans received every day in Montgomery, Alabama.

Rosa grew up in the South hearing stories about slavery and racism, and she experienced it when she went to the old and overcrowded all- black school, where school bus transportation for black children was unavailable. She recalled: "I´d see the bus pass every day...But to me, that was a way of life; we had no choice but to accept what was the custom. The bus was among the first ways I realized there was a black world and a white world" (The Story behind the Bus). Thus, Rosa´s consciousness of the racial inequality led her to disobey and to stand up for her beliefs, but in a civil way.

Reading Rosa Parks´s autobiography I was surprised how this courageous woman, who inspired freedom fighters everywhere, reacted when the bus driver asked her to stand up so that a white passenger could sit. She was quiet, brave and determined. Her husband Raymond was terrified" the white volks will kill you, Rosa" (Dierenfeld 45).

Rosa was arrested and accused of violating Chapter 6, Section 11 segregation law of Montgomery City Code, although she was sitting in the front seat of the ´colored´ section. Nixon and other black leaders in Montgomery bailed her out of jail the next morning. They seized the opportunity of her arrest and began to plan a bus boycott (46).

Under the leadership of Nixon and J.Robinson, an Alabama State College professor and member of the Women´s Political Council (WPC), over 35,000 handbills were printed and distributed throughout the black community announcing a bus boycott

"We must stop these arrests now. The next time may be you, or you, or you...We are, therefore, asking every Negro to stay off the buses Monday in protest of the arrest and trial" (Dierenfield 45). Furthermore, they selected the Montgomery Improvement Association (MIA) to lead the boycott and they elected unanimously Martin Luther King, Jr., a twenty-six-year-old minister of the black middle class Dexter Avenue Baptist Church, to preside over the MIA. Parks recalled in her autobiography *My Story*:" The advantage of having Dr. King as president was that he was so new to Montgomery and to civil rights work that he hadn´t been there long enough to make any strong friends or enemies"(Parks 136).

After a long meeting of black ministers and leaders, a bus boycott was planned on 5 December, and 90 percent of Montgomery´s black citizens stayed off the buses. Therefore, the city´s leaders met to discuss the possibility of extending the boycott until the desegregation of public buses. On this day, the court found Parks guilty and fined her $10, plus $4 costs, but she appealed the conviction (Dierenfield 46).

Montgomery´s black residents were aware of preserving in their boycott. Some rode in carpools instead of buses, while others chose to walk for miles. In addition, the boycott leaders arranged policies to support this civil protest. They provided taxis to drive the boycotters to various destinations for ten cents per ride, the same fare as the bus, what irritated city officials that began to penalize black taxi drivers for helping the Montgomery´s boycotters. However, the boycott continued for months which severely damaged the bus company´s finances. The city lost $ 1 million because, at that time, 75 percent of the bus passengers were black (49). So, the bus company officials met the MIA members to reach an agreement, but in vain. All the demands that the MIA issued requiring that all bus passengers receive courteous treatment by bus operators were not met.

To achieve the boycott´s success, donations came in from across the country. Black churches raised money to support the boycott participants and therefore not to submit to Jim Crow laws. The bus boycott continued in spite of the fact that black citizens were victims of violent acts. Some of them were assaulted on the streets, while others were arrested and accused of loitering when they were waiting for riders. Furthermore, the homes of King and E.D Nixon were bombed as well as four black Baptist churches. King spoke with a tolerant tone to 300 angry black people: "If you have weapons, take them home; if you do not have them, please do not seek to get them. We cannot solve this problem through retaliatory violence. We must meet violence with nonviolence..." (Darby 41).

The city officials obtained injunctions against the boycott in February 1956, and King and 89 other boycott leaders were arrested. King was ordered to pay $500 or serve over a year in prison (Dierenfield 50). He spent, however, two weeks in jail, which inflamed the boycotters and the black community across the nation. Despite all the pressures to defeat the boycott, blacks decided to stay off the city´s buses until the end of segregation on public buses, and they could sit anywhere they wanted. The blacks were, in essence, optimistic that they would attain full integration in public buses since the Brown decision, less than two years old, that declared that the ´separate but equal´ doctrine had no place in public education. It was obvious for the black community that the doctrine had no place in any public facilities.

The process of Parks had taken months in the court until June 5, 1956 when the federal district court ruled in Browder v. Gayle that bus segregation was unconstitutional (51). The boycott even though continued until the case moved on to the United States Supreme Court that upheld the district court´s decision, declaring desegregation on the public buses.

The Montgomery bus boycott was officially ended December 20, 1956. It had lasted 381 days, and it was a huge success. However, integration met with violence. Snipers shot at buses, expressing their objection to the bus desegregation. Four black churches as well as the homes of black leaders in Montgomery were bombed. Seven white men were later arrested for the bombings; they were members of the organization Ku Klux Klan (KKK) that sustained the system of segregation (51). It took months to end the busing- related violence, and the black Montgomerians could ultimately enjoy their new right of desegregated seating. On 21 December, King, Nixon and other black leaders could sit in front of the first integrated bus.

The Montgomery bus boycott was one of the greatest victories of the Civil Rights Movement; it was truly an important start to the movement. One cannot deny the role of Rosa Parks in changing the law in America. Courage was, in fact, her powerful weapon to fight for what is right. She said in her autobiography, *My Story*: "People always say that I didn´t give up my seat because I was tired, but that isn´t true. I was not tired physically...I was not old, although some people have an image of me as being old then. I was forty-two. No, the only tired I was, was tired of giving in" (Parks 116). Her courageous act not to give in, led to a massive bus boycott that changed the course of history.

I wonder how would be the situation of the blacks in the South and especially in Montgomery, if the bus boycott did not success. I wonder also why the U.S. Supreme Court declared desegregation on public buses. Did the Court truly believe in the right of the blacks to be respected on a public bus, or losing 75 percent of the bus passengers for twelve and a half months seemed to be very detrimental to the state´s economy? The second opinion seems, for me, to be acceptable.

Despite many accolades Rosa Parks received during her lifetime, including the Spingarn Medal, the NAACP´s highest award, the great Martin Luther King Jr.Award, and the Congressional Gold Medal, the highest award given by the U.S Congress, she suffered hardships. She lost her job and she left Montgomery due to death threats.

After this long journey of fight to gain racial equality and justice, unfortunately, segregation remained in the South.

2.3 The Little Rock Crisis

A week after the Brown v. Board of Education decision in May 1954, all United States public schools were instructed to integrate. The National Association Advancement of Colored People (NAACP) arranged meetings in the South, were the black population constituted a majority, to inform them about school desegregation. Little Rock, the capital of Arkansas, was a New South community of 107,000 populations, in which the schools planned also for integration (Dierenfield 32).

The Arkansas Gazette, one of the region´s newspapers, reported the intention of the Little Rock School Board to comply with the Brown decision: „It is our responsibility to comply with federal constitutional requirements and we intend to do so when the Supreme Court outlines the method to be followed"(Freyer 16). Indeed, Virgil Blossom, the Little Rock, Arkansas school superintendent, announced a plan for gradual desegregation of the state´s schools. The NAACP branch of Little Rock criticized, however, his plan claiming that it was vague and slow-moving. Daisy Bates of Little Rock, president of the Arkansas NAACP State Conference of Branches, required clear and immediate integration of the state´ s schools (Dierenfield 34).

In addition, the Blossom plan was met with hard reactions from several segregationists. Erving Brown, president of the Capital Citizens´ Council, for example, pointed out that the plan was unnecessary: „The Negros have ample and fine schools here, and there is no need for this problem except to satisfy the aims of a few white and Negro revolutionaries" (32). On the contrary, the school board believed that the Blossom plan did not represent a delay for the schools´ desegregation, but it would comply with the Supreme Court´s ruling.

Opinions varied widely between segregationists and integrationists. District officials decided, therefore, to begin token integration in September 1957 at Little Rock Central High School. Meanwhile, the NAACP filed suit against the Little Rock School District on behalf of thirty-three African American students who were denied admission to all-white schools. The federal courts upheld, however, the school district´s decision arguing that the Blossom plan was reasonable, and it complied with the Supreme Court´s ruling.

With fall of 1957 approaching, school district officials created a system for selecting African American students who sought admission to white only schools. The selection process limited the number of black students focusing on the intelligence, character, and health of the applicants. After accurate interviews with eighty black students, only nine were chosen for Central High School, Melba Patilo Beals, Elizabeth Eckford, Ernest Green, Gloria Ray, Carlotta Walls Lamer, Terrance Roberts, Jefferson Thomas, Minnijean Brown Trickey, and Thelma Mothershed Wair. These African American students, who had been chosen because of their excellent grades, looked for a successful education in the best high school in Little Rock, Arkansas, and they became known around the world as the „Little Rock Nine" (Little Rock Crisis, 1957).

On September 4, 1957, the first day of school at Central High, Orval Faubus, Arkansas governor, defied the court´s injunction and called the Arkansas National Guard to block the "Little Rock Nine" from entering the school with about 2000 white students. A day before, he announced on statewide television that the guardsmen were needed to prevent violence at Central High School, saying,"...they would act not as segregationists or integrationists, but as soldiers called to active duty to carry out their assigned tasks" (Dierenfield 34). A guardsman explained later to a reporter who was covering the Little Rock desegregation crisis that "their real task was to keep the niggers out" (34).

Daisy Bates and some ministers accompanied eight of the students to the school in two police cars, so as to prevent a racial explosion. They were, however, turned away by the National Guard and they were returned home. Unfortunately, the ninth student (15- year-old Elizabeth Eckford) arrived alone at the school and she confronted an inflamed mob of people protesting integration and scramming:" Here comes one of the niggers! Lynch her! Lynch her!" (35). Threatening to kill her, Eckford escaped trembling to the next bus city. She expected, in fact, the guardsmen to protect her. Reporters, who were covering the process of the Little Rock desegregation, described the racial slurs the black students confronted from the segregationists at the school (36). Scenes of the Arkansas National Guardsmen using bayonets to keep all blacks out of the school were pictured in newspapers and polarized the nation.

The ´Little Rock Nine´ were to stay at home for more than two weeks waiting for integration. Observing the embarrassing situation, Judge Ronald N. Davies granted an injunction to NAACP lawyers Thurgood Marshall and Wiley Branton to prevent Governor Faubus from blocking the students´ entry to Central High. Faubus removed, thus, the guardsmen from the school but replaced them with city policemen arguing that he was maintaining order at the school. On 23 September, the ´Little Rock Nine´ returned to Central High School where they were greeted by more than a thousand angry segregationists yelling insults and chanting "Two, four, six, eight, we ain´t going to integrate" (36). The shocking images of angry mobs assaulting black teenagers going to school were transmitted by NBC News.

Fearing not to control the hostile situation, the school administration moved the black students out of the school. The next day, U.S. Congressman Brooks Hays and Little Rock Mayer Woodrow Mann asked President Eisenhower for help. Eisenhower reluctantly spoke from the White House, pointing out that he would order the 1200-man 101st Airborne Battle Group of the U.S. Army´s 101st Airborne Division from Fort Cambell, Kentucky to escort the black students into the school and to preserve mainly the peace and order of the state (37). On the morning of September 25, 1957, the "Little Rock Nine" entered Central High School under protection from federal troops. Unfortunately, the black teenagers were the subject of persecution inside the school. They endured verbal and physical harassment from their white fellows. Furthermore, graffiti were written on the walls of the school that read ´ Nigger Go Home´ (38). Even though the „Little Rock Nine" were aware of the abuse actions they would face at the Central, they expected a glance of respect or kindness. They were really frustrated, but only one of them retaliated. Minnijean Brown dared to dump a bowl of chili on the head of a white student who kept calling her ´ nigger, nigger, nigger.´ She was, therefore, expelled (38).

The other eight students stayed at the Central High School until the end of the school year. Their integration did, however, not continue when Faubus gained the vote of many white segregationists and closed Little Rock´s public schools, arguing that violence would increase. His action of preventing any more desegregation effort in Little Rock schools was declared unconstitutional, and the schools reopened in the fall of 1959 (39). Only three black students enrolled at the Central with white students. They were, however, not welcomed.

No doubt, the "Little Rock Nine" made crucial steps in the civil rights movement. They showed that blacks could fight for their right. Yet, they still had a long way to go to prove the world that all people deserve civil rights. In fact, several African American leaders and lawyers kept fighting and pushed the struggle for racial equality forward.

3 The African American Civil Rights Movement´s leaders

3.1 Luther King

Throughout the world the name of Martin Luther King is met with appreciation and respect. His famous speech "I Have a Dream", delivered on August 28, 1963, became, in fact, a beacon of hope to many African Americans seeking equality and justice.

Reading Luther King´s biography, one finds out how this black leader lived his life looking forward to change the world, believing in the chance for racial equality. Martin Luther King, Jr., was born January 15, 1929 in Atlanta Georgia. His father, Martin Luther King, Sr. was pastor of the Ebenezer Baptist church in Atlanta. Martin entered Morehouse College in 1944 and he graduated in 1948 with a degree in sociology. He then continued his pursuit of knowledge at Croezer Theological in Pennsylvania, where he had the opportunity to study the teachings of Indian spiritual leader Mohandas Gandhi. This latter is known for his concept of non- violent protest. King moved later on to Boston University, from which he graduated in 1955 with a doctorate degree (White 5). In Boston he met his wife, Coretta Scott, who was immensely interested in civil rights. In 1954, King became pastor of Dexter Avenue Baptist Church in Montgomery, Alabama, where Rosa Parks was arrested for her resistance to bus segregation.

As said previously, a group of local ministers formed the Montgomery Improvement Association (MIA) so as to direct the 382-day bus boycott. After some discussion, Martin Luther King, Jr., twenty-six years old at the time, was unanimously elected to preside over the MIA. King was the perfect choice to conduct negotiations with the white establishment. John A. Kirk, Chair of History at the University of Arkansas, points out: "It was thrust upon him in many respects... They needed a leader...King was a neutral choice. He was young and new to town and wasn't a threat" (History). King was, however, surprised to his election as the leader of MIA. He wrote later that the election "caught me unawares. It happened so quickly I did even have time to think it through. It is probable that if I had, I would have declined the nomination" (King 54).

Speaking to an audience of thousands inside and outside Holt Street Baptist Church, was a crucial opportunity for King to fight in words for racial equality which helped him to enter gradually the national scene. He told the audience that" there comes a time when people get tired of being trampled over by the iron feet of oppression" (Sunnemark 32).

After the Montgomery boycott, that ended when the Supreme Court declared desegregation on the public buses, King proved his leadership qualities in setting the issue of racial equality forth. Moreover, King was the president of the Southern Christian Leadership Conference (SCLC), which was founded in 1957 and consisted mainly of black Baptist preachers aiming to fight against racial segregation in the

Southern United States. As a matter of fact, King´s fame and prestige grew in regard to his philosophy of nonviolent resistance to unjust laws. In other words, infusing the civil rights movement with a greater moral purpose, Martin Luther King believed in the power of nonviolence that can be applied to individual conflicts. Indeed, he described six principles of his philosophy of nonviolence in his first book *Stride Toward Freedom.* According to King, the principles of his philosophy consider nonviolence as a way of life of courageous people to resist evil. He states also that nonviolence´s purpose is to win friendship and understanding which creates the Beloved Community, insisting that nonviolence seeks to fight injustice and not people. King assumes that nonviolence prefers love instead of hate concluding that nonviolence believes that God is on his side (King 9). King´s beliefs and actions were, in essence, influenced by Mahatma Gandhi's teaching that jelled with his own Christian beliefs. In other words, King´s inspiration from Mahatma Gandhi played a crucial role in pushing forward his Civil Rights Movement.

As the civil rights movement progressed with the success of Montgomery, the SLLC entered Birmingham, Alabama, which was described as the most rigidly segregated city in the United States, in April 1963.

In February 1960, the civil rights sit-in was born when four African American college students walked up to a whites-only lunch counter at the local Woolworth's store in Greensboro, North Carolina, and asked for coffee. The service was refused and Students from the North and the South came together and formed the Student Nonviolent Coordinating Committee (SNCC) after consulting with King and SCLC leaders.

As far as King´s visit to Birmingham, Alabama is concerned, he was invited by the Reverend Fred Shuttlesworth, leader of the Alabama Christian Movement for Human Rights. Boycotts and sit-ins of downtown stores were to be combined with damaging marches, which forced the federal government to take sides. The police used dogs and water-hoses to attack the demonstrations and these brutal events in Birmingham were shown on television sets all over the world (Sunnemark 41). King was among the hundreds of demonstrators that were arrested and he spent a week in jail where he wrote the famous "Letter from Birmingham Jail".

King´s letter in Birmingham remains one of the classic documents of the civil-rights movement. It was written in response to a public statement of concern and caution issued by eight of the city´s white clergymen, published in the Birmingham News, attacking King and his methods and arguing that the SCLC´s campaign is unnecessary and ill-timed. In his "Letter", King explained the reason of his presence in Birmingham is to battle injustice. Criticizing King and his followers, clergymen described them as 'outsiders´ who cause only trouble in Birmingham´s streets. To this, King affirmed that the black community had no other choice than fighting in the streets believing that all communities and states were interrelated. He states: "Injustice anywhere is a threat to justice everywhere. We are caught in an inescapable network of mutuality, tied in a single garment of destiny. Whatever affects one directly, affects all indirectly… Anyone who lives inside the United States can never be considered an outsider…" (Letter from a Birmingham Jail).

King further pointed out that the black man has waited "more than 340 years" for justice. He explained in detail how his people have suffered until his present day, giving an example of an embarrassing situation with his children when they want to go to the public amusement park. King had only one answer that it is closed to colored people.

In short, King´s "Letter" addressed universal questions of freedom and inequality explaining plainly the concepts of nonviolence and civil disobedience. Indeed, a Newsweek opinion poll announced that" 95% of blacks now regarded King as their most successful spokesman" (White 19).

Furthermore, King´s ideology matured after the successful negotiations of Birmingham, and he demonstrated his oratorical skills during the massive March on Washington for Jobs and Freedom on 28 August 1963. To an audience of more than 200,000 people, King delivered his popular speech 'I have a dream'. He began his

23

speech with a reference to the Emancipation Proclamation that proclaimed the freedom of millions of slaves. He stated, however, that the black man was still not free:

> "One hundred years later, the life of the Negro is still sadly crippled by the manacles of segregation, and the chains of discrimination. One hundred years later, the Negro lives on a lonely island of poverty in the midst of a vast ocean of material prosperity. One hundred years later, the Negro is still languishing in the corners of American society and finds himself an exile in his land. One hundred years later..." (Bennett 120-121).

Toward the end of his famous speech, which gave birth to the Civil Rights movement, King turned his eyes from the paper and he began repeating the rhythmical phrase "I have a dream". The most quoted and remarkable lines of the speech include "I have a dream that my four little children will one day live in a nation where they will not be judged by the color of their skin, but by the content of their character. I have a dream today "(122).

His words, mostly about peace, left a great impact on the crowd who began screaming and crying expressing their excitement and emotion. However, eighteen days after King´s powerful speech, someone threw a bomb into the Sixteenth Street Baptist Church. This latter was filled with Sunday school students. Four girls died and many were injured. At that time, King came to the realization that there was much work to be done if his dream was to come true. On the other hand, Time magazine named in the same year King, Jr. Man of the Year. He was also awarded the Nobel Peace Prize in 1964, and he became the youngest person ever to receive this Nobel Prize.

In the spring of 1964, King and the SCLC selected St. Augustine, Florida, that was preparing to celebrate its 400th anniversary, to start a massive campaign supporting the small local movement to put an end to racial segregation in the oldest city in

America. They organized actually nonviolent demonstrations with the hope of forcing the local authorities to desegregate the city´s public accommodations and institute fair employment policies. However, King and the SCLC faced angry mobs of white segregationists and the Ku Klux Klan. King had to spend again time in jail. On the other hand, the black civil demonstrations could gain international attentions. *Izvesta*, the Soviet newspaper, featured, for example, "a photograph of the violence in St. Augustine and further dramatized the need for passage of civil rights legislation" (White21). King witnessed later the signing of the historic Civil Rights Act by President Lyndon B. Johnson in the White House on 2 July, 1964.

As a leader, Dr. King had the purpose to spread the philosophy of nonviolence. He led thousands of nonviolent demonstrators from Selma, Alabama to the state capital of Montgomery, where the SCLC and Student Nonviolent Coordinating Committee (SNCC) had organized a voter registration campaign. This march came to be known as the Selma-to-Montgomery Freedom March. King told the throng, included more than 25,000 people: "There never was a moment in American history more honorable and more inspiring than the pilgrimage of clergymen and laymen of every race and faith pouring into Selma to face danger at the side of its embattled Negroes" (Selma to Montgomery March (1965)).

That August, President Johnson signed the Voting Rights Act of 1965 in the presence of King and other civil rights activists. In essence, all African Americans guaranteed their right to vote, which paved the way to more civil demonstrations demanding fundamental changes.

King turned his attention to the North, especially Chicago, focusing on the city´s segregated housing policy. He decided then to take the SCLC into Chicago to start a nonviolent demonstration (White 24). King moved, indeed, with his family to Chicago to be closer to the movement, but he had to face Chicago´s mayor Richard J. Daley who was eager to find a way to end the demonstrations. The campaign ended with negotiations promising to build public housing with limited height requirements as well as making mortgages available regardless of race. King confessed that it was the first step in a long journey.

Again King and the SCLC were invited to help striking sanitation workers in Memphis, Tennessee, who were eager to win union recognition. After delivering a speech to the strikers, King was sharply criticized by a Memphis newspaper: "Dr. King´s pose as a leader of a non-violent movement has been shattered. He now has the entire nation doubting his word when he insists that his April project can be peaceful" (29). On 4 April 1968, a day after his speech in Memphis, Tennessee, King was fatally shot by a white sniper while standing on the balcony of his motel.

In short, King´s assassination caused major outbreaks of racial violence in more than 130 cities in 29 states. As a symbol of hope and peace, King´s death induced a mood of regret and sorrow among blacks and whites who welcomed the changes King brought. In fact, Newsweek magazine, which had earlier criticized King´s philosophy, commented:

> "King´s martyrdom on a motel balcony did far more than rob Negros of their most compelling spokesman, and whites of their most effective bridge to black America. His murder, for too many blacks, could only be read as a judgment upon his non-violent philosophy-and a license for retaliatory violence" (30).

Certainly King was an eloquent orator who captured the hearts of people with not only his words, but also with his presence and leadership in marches as well as spending times in jail, fusing the concept of nonviolence to ensure civil rights for all people regardless of race. Likewise, the African-American Muslim minister and the human rights activist Malcolm x is considered as a major twentieth-century spokesman for Black Nationalism. He adopted, however, the notion of violent resistance in the fight of civil rights.

3.2 Malcolm X and Black Muslims

Reading the biography of Malcom X reveals besides his uneasy early life, the contradictory attitudes he was taking in his life. He was born Malcolm Little on May 19, 1925, in Omaha, Nebraska. When he became a member of the Nation of Islam, he dropped his ´slave´ surname and replaced it with the letter X that signifies the unknown. His father, Reverend Earl Little, was a Baptist minister and an organizer for Marcus Garvey's Universal Negro Improvement Association that supported a "back-to-Africa" movement for African Americans. Separated from his family after his father´s death and his mother´s mental disease, Malcolm was sent to reform school. As a child of a broken family, Malcolm held many kinds of jobs, and at the age of 20, he was sentenced to ten years in prison for robbery and breaking(Marable 67).

Malcolm remembered later in his Autobiography, coauthored with Alex Haley, how a Massachusetts state psychiatrist was troubled after interviewed him in prison. He told him that his parents had been preachers and how he was racially insulted when his white mother married to a black man. So, the psychiatrist commented that the prisoner "has fatalistic views, is moody, cynical, and has a sardonic smile which seems to be affected because of his sensitiveness to color" (70). Confronting the challenges of prison life, Malcolm was obliged to behave fiercely than he really was insulting guards and prisoners alike. Later, he was transferred to the Norfolk Prison Colony, built as a model of correctional reform where he was well disciplined and convinced of the value of education.

Persuaded by his brothers and sisters who were members of the Nation of Islam (NOI), popularly known as the "Black Muslims.", the young nonbeliever Malcolm found in this religion the opportunity of achieving dignity as a black man. His sister Hilda affirmed that blacks could obtain their civil rights only through racial separation (78).

As far as the first leader of Nation of Islam is concerned, Prophet W. D. Fard, who, came from Arabia, led this religion in the early nineteen thirties and taught Muhammad his doctrine about "the Caucasian race the religions of Islam and Christianity, as well as the truth about the beginning of creation, the impending destruction of the Caucasian race and its civilization, and the final overthrow of white rule over the black peoples" (Essien20-21).

Malcolm wrote then directly to the Nation of Islam´s supreme leader, Elijah Muhammad, who founded this religion late in the 1930s and he was based in Chicago. Immediately Malcolm received a reply from Muhammad with a five-dollar bill. Influenced by his thesis that considered the white man as the devil, Malcolm joined the Nation of Islam and adopted the name of Malcolm X starting a spiritual journey in life. By early 1950, Malcolm X caused many black inmates to convert to Islam forming a small group that demanded exercising their rights of religious freedom (Marable 93). The prison´s officials decided, however, to transfer Malcolm with many Black Muslims back to Charlestown criticizing his hate to the whites.

Moreover, Malcolm X expressed his opposition to the government's controversial policy by sending a letter to President Truman stating his objection to the Korean War. Marable points out: "It was this letter that brought Malcolm to the attention of the FBI, which opened a file on him that would never be closed. It also marked the beginning of their surveillance of him, which would continue until his death" (95).

After his release in August 1952, Malcolm X went to Chicago to meet Elijah Muhammad; with him he became active in the movement. Later and as assistant minister of the organization, Malcolm directed Temple Number One in Detroit. In March 1954, he was sent to expand the Temple in Philadelphia, Pennsylvania as well as leading the Temple in Harlem (107). Consequently, Malcolm´s successful efforts on behalf of the Nation of Islam grew and he became the most important national spokesman of the organization. While a major movement at this time called for racial integration by using nonviolent methods, Malcolm X and the Black Muslims urged to black solidarity and racial separatism. Thus, rejecting the civil rights movement's strategy of nonviolence, the whites grew fearful of Malcolm X and the Black Muslims´ doctrine.

As the organization reached its peak, Malcolm X brought the attention of the FBI. Indeed, an African-American informant assessed later both Malcolm´s character and his status in the Nation of Islam. He stated that Malcolm is an excellent organizer and speaker, able to convince his followers. He has an utter hate for "the blue eyed devils", but he is too much wiser and clever to make a mistake which make him hard to degrade. The informant went on to say that Malcolm does not violate any kind of laws. He does not smoke or drink (139). As a matter of fact, hundreds of African Americans converted and joined the Nation of Islam. In 1958, Malcolm married Betty Sanders, a young student nurse, who joined the Nation of Islam after attending frequently Malcolm´s lectures and changed her name to Betty X. The couple had six daughters.

Moreover, Malcolm X presented his comments in a 1959 New York City television broadcast about the Nation of Islam in America with a confrontational title, *The Hate That Hate Produced* and broadcasted in five parts. This television documentary was produced by the journalists Mike Wallace and Louis Lomas. So, the show included interviews with Malcolm X, Elijah Muhammad as well as many leaders of the religious group. As the spokesman of the Nation of Islam, Malcolm X clarified to the journalist that all white people were evil. Likewise, Elijah Muhammad, the leader of the NOI, declared that black people were divine and white people were devils asserting that Allah was a black man (Lincoln 69). For Malcolm X, the television documentary had demonized the Nation of Islam. „But parts of Malcolm always believed that even negative publicity was better than none at all"(Marable 162).

The reactions were actually by the side of the Nation of Islam. The program brought, in essence, the organization to a much wider audience. For most white people, it was the first time to hear of the Nation of Islam and the number of people converting to Islam increased remarkably. With the goal of reaching a wider public,

Malcolm X attempted to meet national and international leaders. He met Gamal Abdel Nasser of Egypt, Ahmed Sékou Touré of Guinea, and Kenneth Kaunda of the Zambian African National Congress in the United Nations General Assembly in New York. There Malcolm X met also the Cuban Prime Minister Fidel Castro who was impressed with Malcolm X and he, therefore, repeatedly invited him to visit Cuba.

Malcolm X´s meeting with Castro was nevertheless unwelcomed by the leader of the Nation of Islam, Elijah Muhammad who was fearful of Malcolm´s growing influence that reached even into the respected Student Non-Violent Coordinating Committee (SNCC) (175). So, Muhammad´s support to Malcolm X moved actually back. At the same time, Malcolm X was convinced of Muhammad´s corruption in the organization blaming him lacking in sincerity.

In addition, the political course Malcolm X had consciously followed would quickly lead to his departure from the Nation of Islam. Herman Ferguson, a public school assistant principal known for his activity in leading civil rights demonstrations in Queens, pointed out: „I felt that…eventually Malcolm would have to leave the Nation of Islam. He was just too political…He was developing too fast" (268).

In fact, Malcolm X attempted to forge relationships with established civil rights organizations which made his popularity blowing up. However, he was hardly criticized by the Nation of Islam´s members. Louis Farrakhan, known as Louis X wrote in an article in the official newspaper of the NOI Muhammad speaks:" Such a man as Malcolm is worthy of death, and would have met with death if it had not been for Muhammad's confidence in Allah for victory over the enemies" (World History Project). In essence, Malcolm´s remark about the assassination of President Kennedy was the main incident that led to his suspension from the organization. He declared that the Kennedy´s assassination was a case of „the chickens coming home to roost." He continued offensively:" Being an old farm boy myself, chickens coming home to roost never did make me sad; they´ve always made me glad" (Marable 272-273).

Malcolm´s comment could only suggest that the assassination of Kennedy brought him enjoyment. On the contrary, Elijah Muhammad had already informed all NOI members not to comment in public on the murder of Kennedy, taking into consideration his popularity with black Americans. Therefore, Malcolm X was prohibited to speak for the movement for ninety days. On March 8, 1964, Malcolm X left the Nation of Islam but he remained a Muslim.

Out of the Nation, Malcolm X founded a religious organization, the Muslim Mosque, Inc. believing in the necessity of working with other civil rights leaders. He met, indeed, Martin Luther King, Jr in Washington, D.C as the two black leaders attended the Senate's debate on the Civil Rights bill (302).

At this time, Malcolm X was interested in the orthodox Islam faith of the Middle East after meeting the Muslim professor, Dr. Mahmoud Shawarbi, who played a crucial role in paving the way for Malcolm X to convert to Sunni Islam. He decided then with financial help from his half-sister Ella Little-Collins to make a pilgrimage to Mecca, the Holy City of Islam. There he completed the Hajj rituals and he changed his name to, El-Hajj Malik El-Shabazz. He was also nominated a state guest by the Prince of Saudi Arabia Faisal. During the next months Malcolm visited many Middle Eastern and African countries appreciating the doctrine of Islam that preaches the equality of races, and he, therefore, renounced his earlier racism against whites. Furthermore, Malcolm´s growing fame attracted interest from many African-American activists who welcomed his departure from the Nation of Islam and his participation in civil rights causes.

On the other hand, the conflict with the Nation intensified and Malcolm X was frequently threatened to the extent that his house was destroyed by fire. While Malcolm X on February 21, 1965 was preparing to address the Organization of Afro-American Unity in Manhattan's Audubon Ballroom, a black man fired him twice.

Although one does not know who ordered the death of Malcolm X, but surely Malcolm X was a celebrated freedom fighter who made, with other activists, the struggles of African-Americans an international issue.

At this respect, several artists and writers, including Amiri Baraka, fought with their literary works looking forward to change the world.

4 Baraka´s career as author and black politician

4.1 The former LeRoi Jones

Amiri Baraka was born Everett LeRoi Jones in Newark, New Jersey, on October7, 1934. His parents are: Coyt Leroy Jones and Anna Lois Jones. His father worked as a postal employe and his mother as a social worker. Jones spent a normal childhood, he used to go to see movies on weekends and watch his favorite heroes such as Lone Ranger, and he also used to listen to popular music on radio programs (Hudson 7). His parents were supportive and encouraged him to have his education and do social interaction; he lived a sheltered but ordinary childhood. Baraka said in an interview in 1998 that the main role played by his parents was to protect him, defend him and give him all knowledge he needs as well as the means to go and fight the white people (Ya Saalam). Through his saying one can notice the concrete evidence of the influence that Jones family had on their child who later on became Black Nationalist and activist.

In spite of being a child, LeRoi Jones was conscious of his black color and this made him get a sense of conflict about race. Besides, his expectations of the American culture began to take place. As a child, his parents were not merely protective, but also the teachers who prepared him for the battle against the white people. LeRoi learned the hard lessons of race in America through the experiences that his extended family went through as well as the experiences of his parents. He used to sit on the lap of his grandmother and hear stories about slavery times; he knew about the darkest American history that he did not study at school (Ya Salaam, Black Arts Movement). After graduating from Barringer High School in Newark, where he was a hard working student involved in the school newspaper, LeRoi briefly attended the Newark branch of Rutgers University, and he moved to Howard University where he specialized in the English literature and minored in philosophy. He defines later his experiences at Howard University: "The Howard thing let me understand the Negro sickness. They teach you how to pretend to be white" (qtd. in Hudson, *From LeRoi Jones to Amiri Baraka* 9).

After graduating from Howard in 1953, LeRoi Jones entered the United States Air Force. He expresses his shock after joining the Army, realizing not only the suffering of black people, but also the sickness of the oppressors who suffer by virtue of their oppressions (Hudson 11). As a sergeant, Jones was installed in a Strategic Air Command post in Puerto Rico. He started searching deeply and studying more literature, and he began to conceive of himself as a writer. Jones said that in this period of his life he spent his time trying to finish all of DuBois and Langston's works (Ya Saalam).

Besides the history of literature that he focused on, Jones received another tangible higher education in the mechanics of racism in America. From his protected childhood and then separated college experience, Jones found himself obliged to confront the military bureaucracy and structural racism mechanisms. It was during his short stay at the United States Air Force that he completely understood the pain of racism which addresses the image of the blacks. So, the American hypocrisies had started to be clear to Jones which led him to start reacting toward it. After Jones was sent away from the Air Force and was accused of holding communists tracts, he then started his heavy rebellion against the Western culture.

In 1957, Jones settled in New York's Greenwich Village where he cultivated strong relationships with a number of avant- garde artists whose concepts were completely close to his thoughts. It was in the Village that Jones encountered his first wife, Hettie Cohen, a Jewish woman and with whom he had two daughters. Many wondered at

33

the marriage of the Negro LeRoi Jones and the white Hettie Cohen, for Jones´ anti-Jewish sentiment. He explained later in *Home*:

> "Mixed marriages, etc., take place usually among the middle
> class of one kind or another- usually the "liberated" segment of
> the middle class, artists, bohemians, entertainers, or the otherwise
> "famous." (Liberated here meaning that each member has
> somehow gotten at least superficially free of his history. For the
> black man this would mean that he had grown, somehow, less
> black; for the white woman it means, at one point, that she has
> more liberal opinions, or at least likes to bask in the gorgeousness
> of being a hip, ok, sophisticated outcast…)" (Jones, *Home* 223).

Jones collaborated with Hettie to create a journal called *Yugen*, published from 1958 into 1963, and which was devoted to less known poets from East Village. Moreover, Jones co-edited the literary newsletter Floating Bear which was described as one of the most crucial of all the underground magazines (qtd. in Hudson, *From LeRoi Jones to Amiri Baraka* 15).

Later, Jones founded with Hettie the 'Totem Press' that published works of famous Beat writers like Jack Kerouac and Allen Ginsberg. In addition to editorial works, Jones sponsored jazz concerts and encouraged young musicians who were known for their ´New´ jazz or, as Jones names it, the ´new Black music´(Hudson 17). In short, LeRoi and Hettie developed friendships in the Village. Hettie states:

> "When we started publishing the magazine *Yugen* the house
> became a sort of place where everybody came on the week-end.
> And so we had week-end long parties in which there were great
> exchanges of ideas. LeRoi was really effective in bringing
> together the more intellectual East Coast people like Frank
> O´Hara and the other poets and the painters and the jazz
> musicians."(14)

Furthermore, Jones published his first collection of poems, *Preface to a Twenty Volume Suicide Note*, in 1961. These poems were heavily impacted by the Beats style of self. They were actually an attempt to break the norms and raise the black issues. In 1963, Jones published his criticisms on African-American music, *Blues People: Negro Music in White America*. Later he edited and introduced The Moderns: An Anthology of New Writing in America, which is considered as his great editorial achievement during his time in the Village. Jones´ reputation as a playwright was established with the production of his highly-acclaimed and controversial play *Dutchman*. It was opened on March 24, 1964, in the Village at the Cherry Lane Theatre and continued there until February of 1965. As the best Off-Broadway Play of the year, *Dutchman* won the Obie-Award and it has been revived several times on the stage. The play was also made into film in 1966.

Jones continued writing plays, for instance: *The Toilet*, *The Baptism* and *The Slave*. One writer comments on Jones´ plays at this period: "The LeRoi Jones plays from 1962 to 1964 were more than a beginning of Black Theater. It [sic] was" (qtd. in Hudson, *From LeRoi Jones to Amiri Baraka* 18).

As far as Baraka´s early life is concerned, one can state that 1960 was a remarkable period for Jones. He made a trip to Cuba with his Beat fellow black intellectuals. During this tour, Jones started interacting with Allen Ginsberg; they both expressed their identical opinions about the Cuban government. However, Jones converted later to Marxism and he started to turn away from Beats movement. Later on, in Havana, Jones met other writers who used to call for better social systems. He thus experienced an inner conflict between the lack of action of Beat and his cherished belief of heroic action. He found that those writers were real heroes who were different from the fictitious ones that he used to watch in films. Before he quitted the Beats, Jones used to believe in their theories which stressed that the soul life is more important than the ego's life. But, this theory proved to be challenging as in his prize-winning essay "Cuba Libre." He found that his concepts of Beat lack social action. This was clearly indicated by Jones:

"The poets, or at least one young wild-eyed Mexican poet, Jaime Shelley, almost left me in tears, stomping his foot on the floor, screaming: 'You want to cultivate your soul? In that ugliness you live in, you want to cultivate your soul? Well, we've got millions of starving people to feed, and that moves me enough to make poems out of" (Jones, *Home* 42-43).

The Beat philosophy did not suit Jones as an African American because he found that their writings did not include African American characters in their popular culture. This led him to begin defending the black community and culture. Later on, in the environment of Greenwich Village, Jones started to establish a black movement. During the growth of the literature movement of Greenwich Village, Jones was ready to build the black arts movement. He left the Beats counterculture and left his fellows behind. He thus started to be identified by the black identity using his own terms.

4.2 Baraka as a political activist

In 1965, following the assassination of Malcolm X, Jones left his wife and his daughters repudiating then his former life. He moved to Harlem where he began a completely new life. Jones explained later his sudden move: "It wasn't any sudden thing. It was a developing thing…My work kept changing steadily… It wasn't any kind of abrupt, rational decision. It was based on growing, change- like everything else- until one day the whole thing became unbearable in a physical sense and I just cut out" (qtd. in Hudson, *From LeRoi Jones to Amiri Baraka* 20).

In Harlem, Jones founded The Black Arts Repertory/Theater School stating that the aim of this project is to re-educate Harlem Negros so as to be proud of their blackness (Hudson 21).

Rejecting the Beats theories as well as their style and literary philosophy, Jones started utilizing different structures in his poems to forge a new, clearly African American voice. This was plainly indicated in his collection, *The Dead Lecturer*,

36

which shows Jones´s dismiss of understanding and harmony with whites. The collection is actually an expressing treatment of violence portraying the suffering and torture of the black man. Later on, Jones became interested in the dogmas of the Black Nation of Islam that used to be discussed by Malcolm X. He was mainly influenced by Malcolm X's theories and his ideas that stressed racial confrontation. During his pursuit of revolutionary theories in 1967, Baraka became a "Kawaida minister", he changed his name from "LeRoi Jones" into " Imamu Amiri" (or Ameer) Baraka. "Imamu", is Muslim Swahili name that means "Spiritual Leader," as for the word "Amiri", an Arabic name, it refers to "Prince". "Baraka" is also an Arabic name that signifies "blessings" (34).

In 1966 Baraka remarried to the African American poet Sylvia Robinson, who later became Amina Baraka. They had five children.

Baraka's anger was clearly noticed through his political views and activities; he thus frequently confronted the police as well as racists. During the summer of 1967, racial rebellions broke out in Newark. People destroyed the city attacking citizens and setting fires. The police interfered beating individuals and using tears gas (26). Baraka was severely beaten and then arrested by police officers. He was charged with unlawfully carrying firearms. Baraka complained about the deliberate brutality of the police confirming that he did not know where the revolvers had come from (27). The judge fined him $25,000, but Baraka appealed the case and won.

As head of the new United Brothers of Newark, where more than the half of the citizens were Negro, Baraka aimed to achieve black power politically in Newark. He gives tips to other blacks:

> "You have to control everything of power in your community.
> You say the Urban League is jive. Sure it is. But you had better
> control it. If you don´t, the white boy will. The poverty program-
> it´s jive. We know that. But we better use it or the white boy will.
> Make up your mind about who is going to control what´s going

on in your community…But you´ve got to organize. You can´t
"speechify" things into happening. Organize!" (qtd. in Hudson,
From LeRoi Jones to Amiri Baraka 32).

Indeed, Baraka went on to proclaim later that performing only literary activities made him feel bored. He asserts that in addition to be an artist, one must be a citizen assuming that he put politics first in his life (34).

Supporting the 1970 election of the African American Kenneth Gibson as mayor of Newark, Baraka´s political activities were set on behalf of black people. Gibson stated later:

> "LeRoi is a very dedicated individual, as you probably know.
> When he decides to do something, that becomes a cause. And he
> participates to the fullest. There was never a time in the period of
> the campaign that he could not be called upon for assistance,
> seven days a week and, you know, any time of night. So you
> have to respect a man who dedicates himself to his cause" (33).

As far as Baraka's drama is concerned, it reflected "African socio-dramatic and religious traditions". He borrowed from the African ritual structures and added them to the Black American context. He made use of systems that stress close relationships between the people and their context such as "religious practice and secular events – folklore, ceremonies, or festivals." Moreover, African models appeared in Baraka's Black Theatre Movement. His Black theatre stressed his views against racism; this kind of theatre led to the emergence of Baraka's Black Arts Repertory Theatre in 1965, and" his Spirit House Movers and Players troupe in 1968" (Effiong). The concepts of the Repertory Theatre and Spirit House were based on Baraka's "Black Revolutionary Theatre" in which he revealed his interest in African "socio-artistic values".

After being presented in 1965, Black Revolutionary Theatre indicated Baraka's anti-racism views of the 1960s, which was against the liberal, academic, and

European norms. The Theatre showed the hostility of the whites towards the blacks and it was used as a tool through which Baraka and other intellectuals anticipated the end of the Euro-Americans bourgeoisie. Baraka, as a leader of the Revolutionary Theatre, had a major role in stressing a concrete function of the Black drama, in which he depicted Black survival and struggle (Effiong).

Baraka's revolutionary theater got developed along with his activist movements. He significantly included black music, dance and other tools as essential parts of his drama, he, thus, maintained African rooted elements to make the audience interact with him "emotionally, intellectually, verbally, and physically, much like the traditional African spectator-participant that becomes fundamental part of performance through its choric presence" (Effiong). By including many genres, Baraka's Revolutionary drama managed to create a kind of mutual interactions between the actors and the audience.

Baraka's drama was characterized by bloody ritual that was full of revenge; it was also characterized by a kind of purification of the Black society of the impure White. In this drama, the Whites were destroyed and bloody rites became Baraka's symbol for Black regeneration. This is why "his revolutionary plays were structured on recurring archetypal, thematic, and stylistic traits. Characters were typically allegorical, with White adversaries materializing as beasts or devils" (Effiong) that should be exterminated along with their associates Blacks who did not succeed to get reformed. Baraka's norms indicated that the Whites are evil and the Blacks are good and that good is always victorious. . His theatre is a form of trial where Whites were called and then judged and punished:

> "The functional basis of Baraka's drama was thus situated in a spiritual dimension aroused and sustained through ritual. The communality generated by ritual supported his ideology and retained certain liturgical qualities that derived from his African background. As in African ritual systems, the Revolutionary Theatre did not distinguish the sacred from the secular, ritual

from theatre, or theatre from life. It encompassed the total experience and aspirations of the Black community" (Effiong).

Generally, violence was a main ritual tool used in Baraka's Black dramas. He depicted excessive cruelty towards the Whites; his dramas foretold the change of the Black's situation via determination and perseverance. Baraka expressed, for instance, in his poem *"Black Art"* the need of violence. He declaimed: ´We need poems that kill´ which coincided with the rise of "armed self-defense and slogans such as ´Arm yourself or harm yourself´ established in that period and promoted confrontation with the white power structure, especially the police (e.g., "Off the pigs") "(Ya Saalam).

Baraka's black literature and art have meaning only as acts leading to political awareness and revolutionary action; the aim is the destruction of white America; then in an internationalist perspective, suppression of white domination wherever it exists. To do this, Baraka insisted on breaking the false values first through refusing the White's culture, religion, rationalism and, above all, the myth of the peaceful integration; he also focused on deleting the use of the White society as a reference code by the Blacks. Baraka favored the irrational and magic, the African-American specificity, that is to say, he clarified the urgent need to see himself as Black, understand the world as Black, and change it for the Blacks.

Baraka's greatest contribution to the Black Power movement is his book *Blues People*, where he developed the revolutionary theory that the changing status of African Americans has been reflected in the changes of black music. His social and political reading of blues and jazz has had a major influence in the field of Popular Music Studies (Bracey and Harley).

As a visiting professor, he taught culture and African-American literature at Columbia University and was a full-time professor at Rutgers University. In 1987, he participated with Toni Morrison and Maya Angelou at the ceremony in memory of James Baldwin. In 1998, he played the character of Rastaman in the film *Bulworth* of

Warren Beatty. He received many honors and awards. In 2001 he became a member of the American Academy of Arts and Letters (Bracey and Harley).

Baraka also contributed to the black American music. Blues music was first created by black slaves according to their condition and prohibitions made by their white masters. Baraka thus tackled the Blues, the Negro Spirituals, Jazz, Bop and Hard Bop, but also Rhythm & Blues and Soul. Blues is the subject of his book *Blues People*, it is also an excuse to explain the bath of Blacks in the American society; they came as slaves first, and then became citizens; Baraka explained their social climbing and how they were rejected by the Whites; then they reached a certain level where they were aspiring to look like White Americans. The ambivalence between the poor Blacks and the middle class Blacks was present in this book, and it is interesting to see that all musical innovations were made by the Blacks who were the poorest. Jones calls the book a "theoretical endeavor" that "proposes more questions than it will answer" (qtd. in Hudson, *From LeRoi Jones to Amiri Baraka* 93).

In short, it is interesting to note that Baraka's book *Blues People* came out in 1963 in the United States of America, precisely at a time when the emancipation of people of color in the "land of freedom" began to take a size and growth. It is not only a book on music, but also a sociology book (Bracey and Harley).

Baraka advocates violence as mode for social change. Nevertheless, he insists in an interview with Stone that he is not a violent man, and that is what he is trying to declare in Dutchman (Reilly 10). Baraka stresses actually in his literary masterpiece that the whites really do not understand the blacks.

5 *Dutchman* and *The Slave*: Two plays of race conflict

5.1 *Dutchman*

5.1.1 The play *Dutchman*

Amiri Baraka´s *Dutchman* is one-act play in the 1960s. With its first and successful presentation at the Cherry Lane Theatre in New York City on March 24, 1964, Baraka became famous and respected for the powerful voice he brought to the American theatre. In other words, *Dutchman*, which was the last play produced by Baraka under his birth name, LeRoi Jones, shook up the American theatre scene with ideas and language not heard before.

The theater critic, Harold Clurman, states:

> "*Dutchman* indicates the emergence of an outstanding dramatist-
> LeRoi Jones, His is a turbulent talent. While turbulence is not
> always a sign of power or of valuable meaning, I have a hunch
> that LeRois Jones´ fire will burn even higher and clearer if our
> theatre can furnish an adequate vessel to harbor his flame. We
> need it "(Watts 67).

The play depicts a meeting between a white sadistic temptress woman and a middle class black college student in a New York carriage on the underground in the 1960's. It comments, in fact, on the survival of the Black Man in America which is linked with his ability to keep his blackness and his identity hidden.

Baraka´s play won Award for best off-Broadway play. It ran well into 1965 and turned several cities in the United States and in other metropolises like Paris, Berlin and Spoleto (Italy). *Dutchman*, which exposes the suppressed rage and hostility of American Blacks towards the dominant white culture, is translated into many foreign languages. It has also been filmed in England under the direction of Anthony Harvey, and adapted in France for Jean- Luc Godard´s movie *Masculine- Feminine.*

In New York, however, the intention to the film *Dutchman* was boycotted by subway authorities. A Washington theater complained against a television station which had stopped videotaping a performance of the play, arguing that the language was bad and there is too much kissing.

As far as the play's historical context is concerned, 1964 was a tense year in the United States for civil rights issues. Popular rebellions and protests occurred so as to obtain legalized equal rights for blacks. At the time Baraka wrote his play *Dutchman*, he was part of the Bohemian literary culture of Greenwich Village. Like Clay, Baraka had aspirations as a poet.

5.1.2 The main themes in the play

5.1.2.1 Black man as a victim

In *Dutchman*, the most widely known of Jones' works, the playwright exposes feelings of anger, hatred and guilt through emotional reactions of the two main characters, Lula and Clay. The play takes place on a New York subway car. It opens with Clay, a twenty-year-old middle-class Negro on his way to a friend's party. Clay's name suggests malleability and according to the Oxford Advanced Learner's Dictionary of Current English, a malleable person or character means easily influenced, trained or adapted. (Oxford Dictionary 516) Lula, a thirty-year-old attractive white woman, who sits next to Clay on the subway, is willing to mould him to her wishes and tendencies. She eats delicately an apple and offers a one to Clay. "Eating apples together are always the first step" (Jones 11).

The apple should have been the clue of Lula's intentions, regarding the fruit as the forbidden one. Lula will tempt Clay with it. Furthermore, she tries to seduce him into a black dance; she wears sunglasses, and uses a 'hip' behop language. Clay is fully blinded by her beauty. Throughout the play Lula hints towards the prospect of sex. She laughs loudly, uncrossing and recrossing her legs and claims to know everything about Clay´s life, his place of origin, and his history and sociology. She is even aware of his friend´s names. Clay is total fascinated by Lula´s personality and therefore loves her white world.

In fact, Clay does not think of himself as a black nigger. He believes he can live as an individual in America society, and he repudiates the history of race relations. In other words, Clay does not acknowledge his race and culture. Baraka shows a brilliant style of speech in Clay´s dialogues, which assumes that he is an intellectual poet. Lula asks him who he thought he was in college. He responds he thinks of himself as Baudelaire referring to Charles Baudelaire, French poet, critic and translator, known for his highly controversial and often dark poetry. Clay does not acknowledge his blackness. To Lula, he is a typical middle-class Negro, who is eager to achieve success in America. He wants to be accepted as a part of American culture. However, Ivy League clothes will never hide his blackness. Lula makes fun of him blaming him for rejecting his identity:

Lula. "Boy, those narrow-shoulder clothes come from a tradition you ought to feel oppressed by. A three-button suit. What right do you have to be wearing a three-button suit and a stupid tie? Your grandfather was a slave, he didn´t go to Harvard " (Jones 18).

Lula, representing the white society, remembers Clay of his history of slavery pointing out that he has no place in this world. He does not belong to America where the rights of blacks have been usurped.

As a matter of fact, Baraka states: "*Dutchman* is about the difficulty of becoming a man in America" (Jones, *Home* 188). The middle-class Black Clay tries to become a man. He adopts the appearance and manners of the whites. Nevertheless, Lula does not allow him to be an individual. She describes him as a type of „lukewarm sugarless tea", and "tall skinning black boys with phoney English accents" (Jones 10).

Clay represents an accommodationist, who prefers to live in a white controlled society. He chooses not to oppose his torturer. He accepts, in fact, that Lula imposes her values on him. He is, indeed, a victim of the white society. Baraka assumes through his play *Dutchman* that the blacks are responsible for their victimization since Clay accepts his assigned position in the world and he has no intention to combat it.

Scene 1 ends with Lula's omniscience of Clay's life. She is able to tell his life history by the evidence of his dress, his style of speech, and his intellectual ambitions. Basically, Lula could be any liberal who claims to know all about blacks. How they are, and how they should be. She states that she knows more about the blacks than Clay does. Furthermore, Lula concentrates continually in scene 2 on Clay's "Uncle Tom" stereotype: Lula. "There is Uncle Tom... I mean Uncle Thomas Woolly- Head. With old white matted mane. He hobbles on his wooden cane. Old Tom. Old Tom...You're afraid of white people. And your father was Uncle Tom Big Lip!" (Jones 32- 33).

The young Black becomes the victim of Lula's violent behavior and, therefore, of American's racism. She taunts him with racist terms provoking him to violence. The victim finally answers back and puts an end to his submission to Lula and to all the whites. Clay slaps Lula across the mouth to shut her up. Through his three-page saying, Clay expresses his violence, his anger and his hatred for the whites. One hears the voice of the victim who becomes in this point the hero of the play.

> "Clay. Well, don't! Don't you tell me anything! If I 'm a middle-class fake white man...let me be. And let me be in the way I want... I'll rip your lousy breasts off! Let me be who I feel like being. Uncle Tom. Thomas. Whoever. It's not of your business. You don't know anything except what's there for you to see " (Jones 34).

Clay´s long and uncontrolled speech gives also a short view of the tortured psyche of a Blackman in America. In his famous essays titled *Home*, Jones claims: "...America is a land of victims "(Jones, *Home* 191).

He believes that several kinds of victims live in America tormented by the whites who proclaim to understand the blacks. Clay, for instance, reacts rebelliously. He cannot be free from his history, the heritage of slavery that suggests the necessity of the slave to murder his oppressor. "...the only thing that would cure the neurosis would be your murder "(Jones 35).

Through murder Clay confirms his blackness. He decides, however, not to kill Lula. He chooses to stay insane denying his blackness. Lula stabs him to death with a knife, ordering the other passengers to throw his body off the rain.

The victimization will go on as another young black man gets on at the next stop.

5.1.2.2 Metaphorical Representations for America and the Oppressed

Baraka´s one-act play *Dutchman* is no doubt a literary masterpiece. It deals with black-white relationship in America during the 60´s and can even been related to today´s society. The play expresses many issues, such as: racial tensions, submissiveness, manipulation, cruelty, integration etc. It takes place inside a subway car where a conversation between the two main characters Lula; a thirty-year-old attractive white woman, and the twenty-year-old middle-class Black Clay, escalates from audacious flirtation to tragedy.

Analyzing the metaphorical representations of the two characters in the play requires studying their roles assigned by the playwright in his work *Dutchman*.

The opening scene of the play refers to´ a man´, not to his name Clay, as in many plays of the absurd that present the characters as "puppets rather than persons, body parts rather than full personalities "(Sollors 118).

Clay represents the middle class African American who is eager to achieve success in America, submitting and accepting the white´s false view about blacks. Lula represents, however, the beautiful –seducing woman who attempts to tease Clay leading him to a devilish game that ends with his murder. To conclude that Lula is responsible for Clay´s fate, who represents all African Americans, we must first infer that Lula is America. Baraka assumes that neither Clay nor Lula are symbols. He insists:

> "But I will say this, if the girl (or the boy) in that play has to ´to represent´ anything, I mean if she must be symbolic in the way demented academicians use the term, she does not exist at all. She is not meant to be a symbol-nor is Clay- but a real person, a real thing, in a real world. She does not represent anything- she is one. And perhaps that thing is America, or at least its spirit " (Jones, *Home* 187).

It is obvious that how Lula at the beginning of the play forces herself into Clay´s world. She sits beside him and initiates their conversation about race and sex. Lula is white, which means that she has power. She is America where blacks have suffered centuries from oppression and slavery. She tells Clay:" Lula. I even got into this train, going some other ways than mine. Walked down in the aisle…searching you out " (Jones 7).

Thus, there is a similarity between Lula and America that brought the first African slaves to the New World, considering the title of the play. In spite of the fact that Clay and Lula meet the first time in the subway, she insists that she knows everything about his life because he is a ´well-known type´ and she knows him ´like the palm´ of her hand. This acknowledgement helps us to believe that Lula created Clay´s history, taking into account the slaves´ history.

The connection with Lula representing America as well as being responsible for Clay´s tragedy becomes valid since "The creator of something is always at least partially responsible for that something´s actions " (Metaphorical Representations).

Furthermore, the notion that Lula represents America can only be acceptable because Clay is attracted to the liberal white woman Lula. Whatever she says about herself is supposed to come as a surprise to Clay. "…You sure you´re not an actress? All scribed? There´s no more?" (Jones 27).

Wearing a ´three –button suit and striped tie´ symbolizes also Clay´s assimilation into the white world. Lula incarnates, in fact, the ideal world of which all Americans dream. Clay, who represents the black everyman, believes in the concept of the American Dream which means for him living free from oppression.

In essence, all immigrants from different races hope to live harmoniously together in the New World (America). So, Baraka shows this similarity between America and Lula´s attractiveness permitting the assumption that, there is a connection between Lula (America) and Clay´s tragic fate. In addition, the conclusion that Lula represents America is evident when Baraka intends to present his white character Lula as a hypocritical woman. She tells Clay: "I lie a lot", and she continues smiling: „It helps me control the world" (9). Baraka refers plainly to something else than to a person, who controls the world through lies. He refers to America as he presumes in his famous essays: *Home* that Lula is perhaps America.

On the other hand, *Dutchman* suggests many metaphorical representations of Clay (the oppressed), who represents the middle-class African American. The playwright shows how Clay is fascinated by the flirtatious beautiful Lula. He allows himself to become vulnerable by admiring her whiteness even though he rejects her advances politely at the beginning of the play. Clay, however, goes off towards the end of the play as Lula´s thrusts become more painful. Her racial tone of superiority leads Clay to change his initial fascination to resentment.

Clay is no more docile. Once his rage is vented, he reproves Lula for having false image of blacks. He insists that the blacks are truly sane.

"Clay. My people. They don´t need me to claim them. They got legs and arms of their own…They don´t need all these words. They don´t need any defense…They´ll murder you, and have very rational explanations" (35).

In short, Clay opposes finally his torturer and chooses to rebel like many African Americans who suffered centuries from slavery and suppression and they decided to take action to gain freedom, taking into account the time the play *Dutchman* was written. Thus, Clay represents the civil rights leaders and all African Americans who fought for racial equality in the 1960´s.

Moreover, the ending of the play is significant in convincing us that Clay represents all young African Americans. As he becomes a powerful rebel, Lula stabs him dead and instructs the other passengers to get rid of his body. *Dutchman* ends with Lula looking slowly at another young black man who gets on at the next stop. This allows a repetition of the same plot. Lula will repeat her murderous acts. She declares that she has seduced and killed her victims for years and has a "gray hair for each year and type."

The circular ending of the play requires, therefore, admitting the emergence of another oppressed. The first oppressed Clay has just been killed by Lula, but the cycle is doomed to repeat itself. Hence, we realize that America murdered Clay who represents young African Americans.

Dutchman invokes the biblical fruit of the tree of knowledge in Christian mythology, as Lula enters the train eating delicately an apple at the beginning of the play. Several folktales use the proverbial apple to symbolize temptation, manipulation and knowledge. One connects Lula in *Dutchman* with Eve as the seductress and initiator of Original Sin. There is no doubt that Baraka mentions in his play to the sexual relationship between Lula and Clay. Eating apples with Lula is, however, searching for knowledge. In fact, Clay accepts eating the apple with Lula indicates that he is ready to know her. He wants simply to integrate. He wants to feel equal to the whites. In other words, Clay wants to feel a real American like many African Americans who have dreamt of racial equality in the 1960´s.

This deduction leads to associate Clay with other African Americans, because they share the same trouble. Following Lula´s instructions is, therefore, Clay´s manner to feel American and not just African as long as Lula is (America) who provides the chance of achieving this equality.

During the train ride, when Clay is alone with Lula, he feels accepted. He is not frustrated of feeling inferior. He is, in fact, conciliating with himself, which fascinates Lula.

"Lula. Everything you say is wrong. That´s what makes you so attractive" (18).

However, they realize that they are no longer alone in the subway. Being alone with a white woman was, in essence, a taboo in the 1960´s. A taboo relationship that led to the murder of several Black men.

By analyzing the relationship between Clay and Lula during their train ride, we assume that "Clay´s death is no instance of mere feminine caprice or a random act" (Williams 136).

It is with the collaboration of the rest of the passengers in the subway that Clay´s body is thrown overboard. The reaction of the riders can only reflect their agreement with Lula´s action, which permits the assumption that everyone in the American society is a participant in the murder of Clay (Black man).

5.1.2.3 Identity

Amiri Baraka (Leroi Jones) had with many African American writers explored the theme of Black identity in their literary works. Dutchman discusses it, however, extensively through its character Clay.

The play depicts identity confusion of the middle-class Black Clay, when he allows himself to be picked up by the white liberal woman, Lula. The two engage in flirtatious talk that later becomes blatant. According to Baraka, Clay is a Negro man who lives in New Jersey with his parents. As a college student he thinks of himself as Baudelaire. He does not think of himself as a black nigger, which suggests that Clay does not acknowledge his black race. In the play, Clay is also described carrying a stack of books symbolizing his intellectual interests. Furthermore, Clay´s three buttoned-up suit reveals that he is of middle class and tries to adopt the dreams of the white society. Ignoring Lula´s hostile remarks at the beginning of the play shows also that Clay adopts the behavior of the sophisticated American society. Clay is, in fact, an imitator of whites. One could say that Clay rejects his blackness and therefore he denies his identity.

The playwright seems to declare in *Dutchman* that the survival of the Black man in America requires keeping his true identity hidden. Baraka has also affirmed in "A poem for Willie Best", that the Black man becomes" A renegade /behind the mask. An even/ the mask, a renegade/ disguise" (Williams 135).

The hero has to mask his face in order to get along with the white society. Clay, like many African Americans, who struggle with divided loyalties so as to integrate, wears a white mask to hide his identity as a black man. For him, the manner of dress and living are indeed a way of assimilation into the American society. Clay´s assimilation does not reveal only that he has turned back upon Black people, but it indicates also that he kills his black identity.

In other words, Clay leaves his own culture and follows the oppressor´s culture represented by the white Lula, who loudly shouts at the end of the first scene demanding to ignore their histories and identities:

"Lula. And we´ll pretend the people cannot see you. That is, the citizens. And that you are free of your own history. And I am free of my history. We´ll pretend that we are both anonymous beauties smashing along through the city´s entails" (Jones 21).

However, Lula accuses Clay of imitating white men, describing him a traitorous who discards his racial legacy just to be accepted into the white society. She criticizes Clay´s clothes taking hold of his jacket and shouts:

Lula. "Boy, those narrow-shoulder clothes come from a tradition you ought to feel oppressed by. A three-button suit. What right do you have to be wearing a three-button suit and a stupid tie? Your grandfather was a slave, he didn´t go to Harvard" (18).

Clay replies unsatisfied that his grandfather was a night watchman. It is obvious that Clay tries to escape from his slave heritage. Moreover, Lula dares to say: "Lula. I bet you never once thought you were a black nigger" (19).

She attacks Clay for avoiding his black identity pointing out that his identity as an American is wrong. Lula reminds him that he is black since his grandfather was a slave.

Lula goes to say: "Lula. And you went to a colored college where everybody thought they were Averell Harriman," (18)

Clay expects himself from other black students and declares that his model is the white French poet, Charles- Pierre Baudelaire. Clay´s answer leads us to realize that he wishes to find a new self through the adoption of white manners and values. This new identity Clay seeks has unfortunately nothing to do with Blackness in America. It means merely an eradication of the Black identity.

Baraka attempts in *Dutchman* to discuss the issue of racial dialectic at the level of identity criticizing the African Americans who deny their blackness in order to assimilate into the American society. Indeed, Baraka states in his social essays, *Home*: "The Black Man must idealize himself as Black. And idealize and aspire to that" (Jones, *Home* 248).

According to Baraka, the black person has to value his Blackness to the extent of desiring it. To those African Americans who adopt the oppressor's culture and values instead of struggling for their rights, *Dutchman* attacks them declaring that building a new identity results merely a destruction of the black identity.

Confronted with Lula's mocking insults, accusing him of being an Uncle Tom and directing verbal-abuse to his mother, Clay goes off. He chooses to take his white mask off and to rebel in the name of all of the African Americans. Clay slaps Lula as hard as he can and he bursts into a long and uncontrollable speech that is cited as the pumping Black heart of the Black Art Movement of the 1960's. As Benston points out,

> "Clay stands here as tragic man, naked and alone, facing the mysterious, the demonic, the difficult truth in himself, and the forces that surround and seemingly control him. Here, with all his prefabricated, protective masks of white philosophy, white religion, white language, and white law stripped away, Clay faces for all black people, as if for the very first time, the essential facts of their existence" (Benston 161.)

Clay chooses to be a man facing his tragic fate and he, thus, gives through his explosive speech a short view of the tortured psyche of a black man in America that whites cannot understand him:

> "Clay...I could murder you now. Such a tiny ugly throat. I could squeeze it flat, and watch you turn blue, on a humble. For dull kicks. And all these week-faced ofays squatting around here, staring over

their papers at me. Murder them too…It takes no great effort. For what? To kill you soft idiots? You don´t understand anything but luxury" (Jones 33).

Clay becomes at this point the hero of the play. He controls his actions and asserts, therefore his negritude and identity. He screams at Lula: "Clay. If I´m a middle-class fake white man…let me be. And let me be in the way I want…Let me be who I feel like being" (34).

The black Clay becomes aware that no matter how assimilated he becomes, he is still black. Ironically, the manner of dress, the aping of Baudelaire are all facades that can never hide Clay´s skin color. In fact, Clay´s character turns during his three-page saying from darkness to enlightenment, and this reversal bears a resemblance to what Aristotle named the "recognition" or "change from ignorance to knowledge"(Benston 162).

Clay learns, however, too late, that to be less Negro is not a solution to the Negro problem. He gains then the upper hand, but decides not to kill Lula. It is significant that Clay, in choosing to remain insane by not murdering, he denies his blackness, his identity in spite of the fact that Clay´s distance from his black people will cost him his life.

"Clay. Ahhh. Shit. But who needs it? I´d rather be a fool. Insane" (Jones 35).

Clay is, in essence, Baraka´s spokesman. Only a year after the production of his play Dutchman, Baraka would get rid of his assimilation and start a new black life in Harlem to avoid the fate of his protagonist Clay.

5.1.2.4 Symbolism

Baraka, like every great revolutionary writer, uses symbolism in his literary works to examine the problem of blackness conveying the futility and result of race assimilation. The climax of the play *Dutchman* occurs when Lula murders Clay in a New York subway car. It is not without significance that Baraka chooses the subway as a setting for his play. The train ride is a symbol of time taking into account Clay´s turn from ignorance to knowledge.

In other words, Clay represents at the beginning of the play, the assimilated black African who abandons his racial identity. Towards the end of the play- the end of ride-, Clay´s actions begin, however, to make more sense. Similar to many civil rights activists who stood up and chose to fight against discrimination. Considering the time of the play was written, it is plain that Baraka refers to the racial tensions that heightened in the mid-1960´s.

Symbolically, Lula is associated with Juliet, Tallaluh Bankhead, an American actress, and Lena the Hyena, the world´s ugliest woman in the "Lil Abner" contest. According to Werner Sollors, "Lula is associated with the biblical seductress Lilith, whose function is a man killer. Her name evokes also the association with furies, witches, and vampires "(Sollors 129).

However, Baraka presents Lula as the apple-eating Eve. She enters the subway car daintily eating an apple and she tries to tempt Clay by offering him a one.

> "Lula. (She returns her hand, without moving it, then takes it away and plunges it in her bag to draw out an apple) You want this?
>
> Clay. Sure.
>
> Lula. Eating apples together is always the first step "(Jones 11).

Baraka employs apples as a temptation device. The apple should have been the first clue of Lula´s intentions, regarding the fruit as the forbidden one. Thus, a biblical reference to Adam and Eve is plain in *Dutchman*. Clay´s archetype is, with no doubt, Adam who recalls us the humankind´s downfall into sin. Similarly, Clay is a victim of seduction of the white woman Lula who is the twentieth century Eve. She tells

Clay referring to Adam and Eve´s discovery of their nakedness: "Lula... I saw you staring through that window down in the vicinity of my ass and legs" (7).

As previously noted, Clay´s acceptance of Lula´s apple symbolizes his desire for assimilation into the white society which will cost him his life.

Clearly the symbolism behind the murder of Clay can be concluded in the notion that denying the racial identity is similar in ways to death.

Further symbolism can be seen in the reference to Snow White in the play. "Clay. Hey, what was in those apples? Mirror, mirror on the wall, who´s the fairest one of all? Snow White body, and don´t you forget it" (30).

This reference to Snow White refutes clearly the notion of "black =bad, white=good". The playwright attempts to state that a white woman is not always the fairest. Lula acts as the witch who offers poisonous apples, as well as her mocking words to manipulate her victims. Moreover, Lula constantly eats apples throughout the play. She bites into an apple and throws it away. Later she eats another one laughing and glancing at Clay. It is not without significance that Lula repeats this process. It merely signifies her longing and hunger for life taking into account that Lula represents America. Symbolically, Baraka refers to America that is considered to be one of the greediest countries in the world pointing out its limitless appetite to gain fortune and power.

Baraka uses other symbolism in *Dutchman* to mention Lula´s seductiveness and power. She is described as "a tall, slender, beautiful woman with long red hair hanging straight down her back, wearing only loud lipstick " (5). Women with red hair are, historically, stereotyped as aggressive and powerful. The Greeks, for example, believed that redheads would turn into vampires following their death. There are also prejudices that associate red hair women with fiery temper.

"Lula. Everything you say is wrong. That´s what makes you so attractive "(18).

Throughout the play, Lula changes from time to time her mood without clear reason. In addition to her temperament, Lula is described as an attractive woman and her lipstick´ in somebody´s good taste´ adds a sense of seductiveness. Her deliberate smile and sexual rhythmical shudder as well as the apple, are clearly the devices Lula chooses to seduce Clay.

Baraka seems to claim that the white culture, embodied in Lula´s character, attempts to suppress Black men emphasizing his notion that whites and blacks will never be unified or equal.

Another symbolism in *Dutchman* can be seen in Lula´s bag full of paper books, which represent the written culture of the white man. Clay carries also a stack of books symbolizing his desire to fit in with the white culture, an oppressing culture.

It would be a mistake, however, not to see the symbolism of the play´s title. Reading *Dutchman* as a mythic drama alludes to the legend of the ghost ship, *The Flying Dutchman*, which is implied in the title of the play *Dutchman*. The playwright underlines, indeed, this connection in the opening of the play: "In the flying underbelly of the city. Steaming hot and summer on top, outside, Underground. The subway heaped in modern myth "(3).

The legend of *The Flying Dutchman* is said to have started in 1641, when a Dutch ship sank off the coast of the Cape of Good Hope. According to folklore, this ghost ship can never go home. It is doomed to sail the oceans forever. It is also said that the ship´s captain was struggling to round the Cape of Good Hope in the Teeth of a terrible gale that threatened to sink hos ship and the passengers. The sailors warned the captain to turn around, but he was stubborn and he refused to change the course (The Legend of the Flying Dutchman).

Clay´s fate parallels the captain and his stubbornness. *Dutchman´s* protagonist Clay seeks acceptance through assimilation into the white society that costs him his life; similarly, the captain in the legend died when he refused to change the ship´s course.

Thus, the similarity between Baraka´s play and the myth is particularly seen in the hopeless ending of the play.

Furthermore, the implication of the title seems plain that Lula is likened to a ghost ship. Her infinite repetition of the murderous actions suggested by the circular ending bears a resemblance to the ghost ship which is, according to folklore, doomed to sail forever.

Lula in the play is a captain and the passengers are the crew who submit to her commands. She controls the situation as Sherley Anne Williams states: "cruising the city´s underbelly, asking Black men the question, which side are you on? And murdering those who, like Clay, respond, My own "(Williams 136).

Williams´ argument echoes that if Clay had continued to submit to Lula´s instructions, she would have let him live. He would not be, therefore, out of the game.

Historically speaking, the title of the play is significant taking into consideration the background of the slave trade. Indeed, Dutch slave traders brought the first African slaves to the New World. "For it was a Dutchman, a Dutch man-of war, which brought the first Black slaves to North America. America symbolically comes full circle through Lula´s –the Dutchman´s- murderous action…" (136).

5.1.3 Gender Roles in *Dutchman*

Dutchman holds more significance than the chance encounter of a black man and a white woman on a subway. It is worth examining the characters of the play classifying their masculine and feminine roles. Baraka presents Lula ten years older than Clay. There is, indeed, a reference to her age in her comment: "Lula. My hair is turning gray. A gray hair for each year and type I´ve come through" (Jones 13). Being older than Clay can merely symbolize Lula´s omniscience as well as her mastery she assumed throughout the play. She is perceptive to the point of

58

omniscience. Lula seems to know everything about Clay's life, and his history and sociology. She is even aware of his friend's names. In other words, Lula's knowledge of stereotypes allows her to guess a lot of things about Clay. In Baraka's own words, "Lula is ´a better critic´ than Bosley Crowther(who reviewed *Dutchman* for the New York Times) and says ´essentially true things´ to Clay "(Sollors 124).

As a matter of fact, the white American society, exemplified by Lula, ignores the black man and knows only the old negative stereotypes regarding him as criminal, drug addict and rapist. These judgments bring the black people down and deny them access to social balance and equality within white society.

In addition to her omniscience, Lula's role in *Dutchman* suggests female control as the male protagonist Clay who submits rather than orders. In essence, Lula is considered to be the dominant partner in the subway, the world of the play. It is she who initiates the conversation by introducing herself to Clay. Even she gives him step-by-step instructions on what to say insisting to use her exact lines and to cut his ´huh´s´.

> "Lula. Now. You to me, Lula, Lula, why don´t you go to this party with me tonight? It is your turn, and let those be your lines.
>
> Clay. Lula, why don´t you go to this party with me tonight, huh?
>
> Lula. Say my name twice before you ask, and no huh´s.
>
> Clay. Lula. Lula, why don´t you go to this party with me tonight?" (Jones 16).

Following Lula's commands does not only symbolize Clay's passiveness, but it indicates also that Lula forces him to take one step back from his identity, his manhood and therefore achieving the same rights as the whites. Moreover, Lula's authority is -until stereotyping Clay Uncle Tom- supreme and unchallenged throughout the play. She keeps control in their confronted conversation by switching constantly topics. In fact, the white Lula entices, rebuffs, analyzes and insults Clay. She makes sure that she controls the conversation.

Another role Lula plays in *Dutchman* is the role of a stalker who is waiting patiently for his prey. Lula stars at Clay through the subway window smiling at him to call his attention. He responds, however, to her deliberate smile with a nervous grin. Lula sits next to Clay employing her sexuality by eating daintily an apple that identifies her as a temptress.

Lula´s chase of Clay will end with his death which is according to Williams, "no instance of mere feminine caprice or a random act" (Williams134).

It is important to keep in mind that *Dutchman* was written during the height of the Civil Rights Movement of the 1960´s in the United States. Baraka depicts the everyday reality, in which white people commit crimes against black people. The play ends, indeed, with Lula spotting her new prey, another young Negro, who enters the train. Sollors describes Lula as" a bookkeeper of murder, who keeps a record in her notebook of the ´contracts´ she has fulfilled" (Sollors 128).

Furthermore, the role of the white female as the seductress is evident when Lula constantly asks Clay to ´rub bellies´ with her and ´knock stomachs´, as well as the proverbial apple she uses to tempt him. Lula reduces, in fact, Clay to a sexual object so as to fulfill her stereotypical beliefs. Representing the mainstream American ideology, Lula sees the black body as a commodity; she can consume it the way she pleases. As said above, Lula´s upfront sexuality is exemplified by the way she acts towards Clay.

It should not be forgotten that Lula also plays the role of a provoker. With her recurrent provocations, she turns Clay into an angry revolutionary who shows his rough side. Lula is who stimulates Clay to reveal issues that must have been closely hidden in the most profound place in his heart (Williams 140). In other words, Lula is responsible for Clay´s explosion as she mainly brings the conversation to the issue of his manhood. She encourages him, in fact, to stand up and his mask finally falls down. Clay faces and threatens, therefore, the white society:

"Clay. They (Black people) will cut your throats, and drag you out to the edge of your cities so the flesh can fall away from your bones, in sanity isolation" (Jones 36).

As I mentioned previously, Baraka depicts Clay´s passive personality represented in admitting what Lula thinks and says. In fact, Clay acts and looks cool, performing this strategy in order to stay out of trouble. Reprimanded for being assimilationist, phony and middle-class white man, Clay does not react at first. His coolness does not allow him to respond to Lula´s affirmation in their confronted conversation:

> "Lula. A union of love and sacrifice that was destined to flower
> at the birth of the noble Clay Clay Williams. Yet! And most of all
> yea yea for you, Clay Clay. The Black Beaudelaire! Yes! (And
> with knifelike cynicism.) My Christ. My Christ.
>
> Clay. Thank you, ma´am.
>
> Lula. May the people accept you as a ghost of the future. And
> love you, that you might not kill them when you can.
>
> Clay. What?
>
> Lula.You´re a murder, Clay, and you know it. (Her voice
> darkening with significance.) You know goddamm well what I
> mean.
>
> Clay. I do?
>
> Lula. So we´ll pretend the air is light and full perfume.
>
> Clay. (Sniffing at her blouse.) It is" (20-21).

These lines indicate a clear evidence of Clay´s coolness. He responds to Lula´s mockery and cynicism in an unaffected manner pretending ignorance of what she is talking about. Performing this acting cool can only denote Clay´s option of not confronting with Lula. Besides, Clay rides a subway full of white passengers with whom he avoids any conflict. In other words, Clay, like many African Americans in the sixties, is aware of the obstacles and tortures imposed upon black man by the white society. He chooses then to adapt cool so as to avoid trouble with the white oppressive society.

Indeed, keeping cool leads Clay to be tolerant, putting up with Lula´s abusive statements. Being tolerant is merely another role Clay plays in *Dutchman* representing the good, while Lula is the evil who insults and manipulates. Clay´s tolerance occurs clearly in the following lines:

> "Lula. I bet you never once thought you were a black nigger.
> (Mock serious, then she bowls with laughter. Clay is stunned but after initial reaction, he quickly tries to appreciate the humor. Lula almost shrieks) A black Beaudelaire.
>
> Clay. That´s right" (19)

However, the roles of the protagonists have been totally reversed at the end of the play as Lula brings the conversation to the issue of Clay´s manhood. As a matter of fact, Clay stands up and affirms his identity stating that everything Lula sees is an act; the cool black boy and his assimilationist behavior are both lies; an act to protect himself from the white power. Sollors points out: "Lula was the protagonist of the play. Clay now becomes the hero. As he drops the bourgeois masquerade, he assumes the role of Baraka´s more contemporary mouthpiece" (Sollors 126).

Lula does, in essence, control the situation guiding Clay in the extent of addressing his inner self raising the issue of his manhood, which empowers him to wake up and to scream at white people controlling, therefore, his action and his language:

"Clay...Don´t you tell me anything! If I´m a middle- class fake white man...let me be. And let me be in the way I want" (Jones 34).

5.1.4 The language in the play

Black artists in the throes of the civil rights struggle, like LeRoi Jones, were voicing their rage in expressionistic art. Reading *Dutchman*, for example, one comes across an uncanny language that is sometimes movingly poetic and sometimes ordinary to the extent that is incoherent, admitting surely that the play is rooted in symbolism. In fact, Lula´s monologues are beautifully uttered giving sense of a poetic dimension.

The following lines denote Lula´s refined and poetic speech:

> "Lula. My hair is turning gray. A gray hair for each year and type
> I´ve come through.
>
> Clay. Why do you want to sound so old?
>
> Lula. Bit it´s always gentle when it starts. (Attention drifting)
>
> Hagged against tenements, day or night "(Jones 13).

Therefore, Lula is clearly in control of the conversation and the situation as she utilizes an effective and a powerful language reinforcing her dominance over Clay. Much more importantly, Lula controls Clay´s language by scripting their conversation and ordering him to use the exact lines: "Lula. It´s your turn, and let those be your lines "(16).

Lacking a convenient language to defend his dignity and his thoughts as a black man in America, Clay remains powerless allowing Lula overwhelming him successfully.

In short, the nature of Lula and Clay´s conversation suggests, thus, a language in which racism is almost inevitable.

On the other hand, Baraka employs ordinary language that consists of the flow of words and idioms used from Lula and Clay in their conversation, which emphasizes the notion that language is strongly present in the play. In other words, Baraka indicates that the words in *Dutchman* speak louder than the actions of the characters. If we exclude the action of Clay's murder, there is no powerful and noticeable action that remains entrenched after reading the play, except the words or language between the two characters. Kimberly W. Benston states: "Indeed, to a great extent we can describe the action of *Dutchman* with Pirandello's phrase, *L'azione parlata*: action-spoken or action- in words " (Benston 154).

Therefore, it is words or language that directs the characters and their actions shaping apparently their identities. The playwright portrays in *Dutchman* how the characters are capable of changing their thoughts and identities when they change the type of language they utilize. There is, indeed, inflections in their speeches related to the change of thoughts and acts. One gets the sense that disorder characterizes the language of the play appeared in the random phrases and the unfinished sentences said by the characters.

Baraka explores through *Dutchman* the problem of communication according to racial differences. He conveys that incoherent language obstructs communication between the characters Lula and Clay, which reinforces the notion of the impossibility of whites and blacks' unity. Furthermore, if we analyze Lula's language, we notice a kind of suppression in the words she uses aiming to understate Clay. As a matter of fact, Lula and the white American society she represents, keep their power and control over African Americans by stereotyping them through statements that place them in an inferior position. Examples of the stereotyping of the black body in a negative way, ca be seen in the following terms of 'liver-lipped', 'boy', and 'Uncle Tom'. Lula calls Clay "…you liver-lipped white man."

Lula employs the adjective' liver-lipped' pejoratively to name the way African Americans' lips are colored so as to bring Clay's moral down. What is more, Lula degrades Clay by calling him a ´white man´, but featuring a ´liver-lip´. Besides, Lula disparages Clay to the level of not being mature when she calls him ´boy´, and she proceeds:

"Lula. You look like you been trying to grow a beard…You look like you live in New Jersey with your parents and are trying to grow a beard " (Jones 8).

Lula emasculates Clay by describing him as a child and not as a man. She uses, in fact, humiliating words so as to injury his dignity and in somehow to take his manhood away.

Moreover, African American men are classified in old stereotypes like Uncle Tom who symbolizes compliance and submission. Lula teases Clay and accuses him of being an Uncle Tom:

> "Lula…There is Uncle Tom… I mean, Uncle Thomas Woolly-
> Head. With old white matted mane. He hobbles on his wooden
> cane. Old Tom. Old Tom. Let the white man hump his ol´mama,
> and he jes´ shuffle off in the woods and hide his gentle gray head.
> Old Thomas Woolly- Head " (32).

Lula perceives in Clay a compliant slave who betrays the African American cause. So, the stereotyping of the black body as well as the way Lula uses language are not only racially charges, but also a strategy used to castrate Clay psychologically making him to rethink before getting involved with a white woman.

Clay responds, actually, to Lula´s abusing and provocative language when he changes his language. He changes, thus, his perception of the reality that he will be never accepted into the white society. He orders Lula:

"Clay. Now you shut the hell up. Just shut up…You don´t know anything. So just keep your stupid mouth closed." He goes on to say: "…let me talk "(33).

Clay bursts into a long speech that can be considered as the most brilliant piece of the play, because it expresses the roiling anger that many African Americans are afraid to admit publically. Benston states: "Clay´s speech is thus a major epiphany of nature itself, of the very ground of black self-awareness, black power, and black freedom. It deserves to be isolated both a Clay´s vehicle for self- discovery and as a Barakan manifesto of black liberation" (Benston 164).

In essence, Baraka asserts the failure of communication between blacks and whites. He seems to imply that black people need to use a new language to fight against the white´s oppression imposed upon them. Clay is presented as an example, whose voice for the struggle of his black society costs him his life.

Differently from Clay, Walker in Baraka´s play *The Slave* leaves aside the talking and decides to take action by leading a violent murderous black rebellion.

5.2 *The Slave*

With *The Slave*, which opened on December 16, 1964, at the St. Mark´s Playhouse, New York City, Baraka continues exploring the theme of tension between blacks and whites in The United States he already presented in *Dutchman*.

5.2.1 The main themes in the play

The Slave was written after the masterpiece *Dutchman*, and it is described as ´A Fable in a Prologue and Two Acts´. In the prologue Walker Vessels appears as an old white-haired field slave dressed in ragged clothing and he briefly introduces the play:

> "Whatever the core of our lives. Whatever the deceit. We live where we are, and seek nothing but ourselves. We are liars, and we are murderous. We invent death for others. Stop their pulses publicly. Stone possible lovers with heavy worlds we think are ideas...and we know, even before these shapes are realized, that these worlds, these depths or heights we fly to smoothly, as in a

dream, or slighter, when we stare dumbly into space, leaning our eyes just behind a last quick moving bird, then sometimes the place and twist of what we are will push and sting, and what the crust of our stance has become will ring in our ears and shatter that piece of our eyes that is never closed " (Jones 43).

Walker, the central character, attacks the whole nature of society blaming it turning people into murders and liars, seeking their selves and their identities. It is plain that Baraka instills his anger and his rebellious nature into Walker character. The playwright examines, therefore, the themes of search of identity, racial hatred and black revolution. In the prologue, which is considered as a long stream- of-consciousness monologue (Effiong 102), Walker portrays precisely his ambiguous existence. He proclaims that the ´core´ and the façade of his life are unclear, and he lives in a dilemma as a slave seeking ´nothing but´ himself. Furthermore, Walker´s elusive identity is clearly stated when he says: "Walker. I am much older than I look…or maybe much younger "(Jones 44).

His age is undefined ´full of great ideas´. He goes on to demand us to distrust our habitual perceptions: "Walker. But figure, still, that you might not be right. Figure, still, that you might be lying…to save yourself "(44).

Walker´s monologue ends with an old blues song that argues self-determination: "Walker. Man, oh, nigger, nigger, you still here, as hard as nails, and takin no shit from nobody "(45).

Thus, singing some blues, Walker transforms himself into the Black revolutionary, who leaves his troops in the battle against the whites, and finds himself in the home of his former white wife Grace and her new white husband, Brad Easley, Walker´s former professor.

Walker and Grace had separated because of their different perceptions. Walker chooses to be a leader of an armed Black liberation movement that proclaims its hatred of whites. However, Grace cannot understand Walker´s transformation from an academic intellectual and poet to militant preaching the murder of all white people. She reminds him that she is white but he replies: "Walker. I was crying out against three hundred years of oppression; not against individuals "(72).

In fact, Baraka´s decision to stay with the Black side is plainly reflected in his play The Slave, in which Walker Vessels decides to achieve liberation for blacks after leaving his white wife and his two daughters. Baraka recalls in his *Autobiography*: "I was stretched between two lives and perceptions (I ´ve told you it was four Black Brown Yellow White- but actually it´s two or the real side, the two extremes, the black and the white, with the middle two but their boxing gloves)" (Baraka 49).

Throughout the play, sounds of explosions are constantly heard which indicate that the blacks are bombing the city and destroying the country. I think it would be unworthy discussing the issue of hatred in *The Slave* without mentioning to Baraka´s famous essay, *"The Revolutionary Theatre"*, which is published in 1965. The central subject of racial hatred is plain in his essay: "White men will cover before this theatre because it hates them…The Revolutionary Theatre must hate them for hating…The Revolutionary Theatre must teach them their deaths" (Jones, *Home* 210-211).

In addition to the fierce verbal battle between Grace, her husband Easley and Walker, this latter comes to the realization that social protest is not enough, and he has to take action. He slaps, indeed, Easley several times pushing the gun into his stomach. Walker kills his white oppressor and, therefore, his whitened past. He sates: "Walker…right is in the act! And the act itself has some place in the world…it makes some place for itself" (Jones 75).

Walker insists on the necessity of rebelling and acting against the white society. One realizes that *The Slave* takes place in the future. It calls, indeed, for a revolutionary future based on violence in the name of Black liberation.

5.2.2 Walker as a leader of the blacks

The Slave holds the subject of understanding is not possible between blacks and whites. We learn in the play that Grace had left Walker years before, because of his increasing Black Nationalist commitments. Baraka insists that Whites can never understand the black man:

"Walker. You can´t understand me" (Jones 66).

Therefore, the play makes the point that the black man and the white woman are not supposed to have any connections, arguing that it was and (is) the huge taboo of the society. Consequently, Walker is tired of so much talking about the oppression imposed upon the blacks centuries ago. He decides to act and to lead an army revolution against the whites. In fact, Baraka claims in his autobiography, published after his trip to Cuba, "It was not enough just to write, to feel, to think, one must act! One could act" (Baraka 166).

Baraka depicts the philosophical change he was undergoing, and this is really what Walker Vessels in *The Slave* is aware of. He decides to take action by killing first his ex-white wife and her husband. Moreover, waging direct war against the white society comprises another concept more than shouting hatred to the whites. It aims at breaking from slavery and its impact on the blacks. As a matter of fact, Walker, the field slave, does not accept to stay passive. He has reached what Baraka was directing to do: "We are self-conscious now, because we are slaves trying to break from slavery. Trying to destroy slavery in the world and in our minds…then there would be no pause, no rhetoric, only action which is divine" (Baraka, *Raise* 147).

The black revolutionary Walker Vessels believes, therefore, that history develops through change and this latter can only be realized through action. He kills his white past and becomes a man without history that reminds him of his slavery. Grace and her white husband Easley opposes, nevertheless, Walker´s revolutionary intentions and they see no need for a radical and bloody revolution. Easley asks Walker if he thinks that blacks could govern the society in a fairer manner. Walker cannot judge blacks superior to whites. Instead, he argues that whites have already had their chance, and now blacks have the right to have theirs. In essence, Walker's answer implies that Baraka does offer his character no alternative to violence and murder in order to fight against the white oppression. Barak's essay "*The Revolutionary Theatre*" interprets, indeed, *The Slave* as a revolutionary play, exhorting the black man to be a stone revolutionist: "Do not let them (white people) swear our leaders, do not let them enter into this community with their bullshit integration fairytales. Remember, you are at war with the devil himself" (Jones, *Home* 236).

After breaking into the home of his former white wife and her husband, Walker holds the gun during the long night insisting that he has come to take back his two daughters. The Easleys and their unexpected guest discuss about the purpose of war and many aspects of their past. The black leader Walker becomes increasingly drunk, but affirms that he will do anything to fight and die for his cause. His troops arrive, indeed, in the city and begin to shell it. The debate continues and the black man expresses his sheer hatred toward the whites, arguing that he has chosen to promote a bloody rebellion knowing "I have killed for all times any creative impulse I will ever have by the depravity of any murderous philosophies" (Jones 66).

On the other hand, Walker's revolutionary intentions are suspect when Easley asks and challenges him: "Well, what the hell do you want, hero?" (48).

Both Grace and Easley refuse to believe in Walker's militant rebellion mocking him as a 'nigger murder'. In addition, Easley wonders how a killer can love his two daughters. Walker states that he still loves them in spite of the fact that he is responsible for conducting a bloody war against the whites. Such a paradoxical justification can merely indicate Walker's ambiguity.

5.2.3 Walker as a victim

Reading *The Slave*, one realizes that Walker Vessels is not able to completely sever his ties with his past. The oppressed man decides, therefore, to revenge and to charge which reinforces the concept of the Revolutionary Theatre that "must Accuse and Attack anything that can be accused and attacked. It must Accuse and Attack because it is a theatre of victims" (Jones, *Home* 211).

Indeed, Baraka asserts that his protagonists Clay, Ray and Walker in the plays *Dutchman*, *The Toilet* and *The Slave* are all victims (211).

In other words, Baraka makes the black oppressed Walker a victim, not only of the white society, but also a victim of his own views. Employing a Prologue in *The Slave*, in which Walker appears as an old slave, signifies plainly the diverse ambivalences that the black revolutionary Walker embodies.

We agree that Walker Vessels is a contradictory character who believes on one hand in the necessity for change through revolutionary means, but he prefers on the other hand not to be in the battlefield so as to lead his troops. He breaks, instead the Easley´s home to ´rescue´ his mulatto daughters. Baraka criticized Walker in a later interview:

> "Walker Vessels suffers from an ego-worship. He´s hung up in his own ego syndrome, his individualism. That´s why I call the play *The Salve*, because if he is the general, the commander of this revolutionary army, he has no business being in that white man´s house: He has no business there talking to these people. He is supposed to be out leading his brothers. He is supposed to be fighting, he´s not supposed to be sitting there bullshitting with white people. And this is why, essentially, Walker is a weak man" (Sollors 137).

The playwright states that Walker is enslaved by the idea of being the one who will accept 'no other adviser except his own ego' (Jones 66).

Moreover; Walker´s mind is not at ease concerning the revolution he has attempted. He cannot, in essence, free himself from his sentimental ties with his former white wife and his daughters. For Walker, Grace is a part of his past that he has thought buried. Although she tells him that she has only pity for him calling him a nigger, Walker is still emotionally attached to her. One can detect ambiguity in Walker´s character, for he has returned to take his daughters in spite of the fact that he has revealed his hate for all white people. It is with no doubt that Walker, who is the black man, who is Baraka, is forced to hate because of the repulsive indignities and the oppression accumulated for centuries on the black man.

In short, *The Slave* suggests that the black man destroys the whites, but he is himself destroyed because he is incapable of loving. Walker thinks that he achieves freedom through rebellion. He is, on the contrary, enslaved by his own hate. The belief of hatred is received and returned. So, the play ends circularly with the central character, Walker, reverting back to the old field-slave who appeared at the beginning of the play.

In addition, Baraka presents in *The Slave* Walker´s paradoxical political view. Although he calls for violence and revolution, he acknowledges that the bloody rebellion he is leading is completely futile. He assumes that this war "will only change the complexion of tyranny "(66). Walker goes on to say that his officers in the battle "are ignorant mother fuckers who have never read any book in their lives," (67).

So, Walker admits clearly that the revolution against the whites will bring no effective change, no liberation. The victim black man would remain a victim. Werner Sollors observes contradictions in Walker´s political position:

"Instead of developing a political concept of Black liberation, Vessels merely follows the impulses of his own love-hate emotions, which he expresses with an insistent *larmoyance*. This flaw reduces Vessels´ political potential to a nihilistic form of action-for-action´s-sake. However, although Walker has no hopeful vision for a revolutionary future, he is fully aware of the mistakes of the liberals in the present "(Sollors 136).

The Slave depicts Baraka´s own view about the ineffectiveness of an armed rebellion to achieve liberation. This latter can be also fulfilled by the language used by the playwright of the Black Theatre Movement.

5.2.4 The language in *The Slave*

The writers in the Black Arts Movement tried in the 60s to bring forth the issue of race, expressing their rage and violence reflected in the language they used in their literary works. Believing that language is the effective expression of a culture, Baraka assumes in his collection of essays, *Home*: "The words of a language become something specific related to their individual users, but for the same reason, each culture has got its own language, because they have their own experience…" (Jones, *Home* 166-168).

The Slave, then, suggests the experience of one´s culture in using a language that becomes the main outlet for rage. This belief is clearly stated in the play when Baraka elaborates that "brown is not brown except when used as an intimate description of personal phenomenological fields. As your brown is not my brown, et cetera, that is, we need, ahem, a meta-language. We need some thing not included here" (Jones 45).

The call for the need of the creation of a new language, whose words have power in the extent of defining one´s perceptions of self and of race reality, was one of the essential goals of the African American writers of the 1960´s in The United States.

As a matter of fact, Vessels in *The Slave* decides to adopt a new language after being fully aware that he has been speaking a language, which does not belong to him: "But almost none of them are mine" (53).

So, exchanging communication with the Easleys is any more possible. Baraka depicts from the beginning of the play the fierce confrontation of Walker and the Easley´ linguistic attacks:

> "Easley. (…)Is that why you and your noble black brothers are killing what´s left of this city? (suddenly broken) I should say…what´s left of this country…or world.
>
> Walker. Oh, fuck you (Hotly) fuck you…just fuck you, that´s all. Just fuck you! (keep voice stiffly contained, but then it rises sharply)
>
> I mean really, just fuck you. Don´s goddamnit, don´s tell me about any goddamn killing of anything "(49).

These lines echo the impossibility of communication and, therefore, understanding between Walker and Easley. They cannot, in fact, progress in their dialogue. Each opposes the other believing that their debate is futile, which leads to Easley´s death. The play suggests, thus, dramatic actions but simple language. Moreover, slurs and street language are present in *The Slave*. However, Walker comes to the realization that insults are not enough. He chooses to adapt a new language, which is simply action and that according to him, it will assure his survival. The playwright portrays, indeed, the act of Easley´s death as a self-defense when he throws himself on Walker.

Consequently, *The Slave*, one of the Movement plays, emphasizes the issue of violence instead of words as an expression of hatred. In his famous essay, The Revolutionary Theatre, Baraka outlines: "We will scream and cry, murder, run through the streets in agony, if it means some soul will be moved, moved to actual life understanding of what the world is, and what it ought to be "(Jones, *Home* 213).

As far as Walker and Grace´s communication is concerned, one notices the exchanging accusations between them through the language they use. Just beyond these accusations lies the aim of using language as a tool for wounding the other. Grace screams and repeats four times that Walker is insane, asserting that he is out of his mind. She is, nevertheless, not able to hurt him linguistically:

> "Grace. I wish I could call you something that would hurt you.
>
> Walker. So do I
>
> Grace. (Wearily) Nigger.
>
> Walker. So do I" (Jones 85-86).

Walker´s triumph over the Easleys in their verbal battle reinforces somehow his superior position in the war he is waging against white society.

Furthermore, the Black Nationalist Baraka employs music in *The Slave*, which conveys its quality to Vessels´ speech and nature. Throughout the play, Vessels´ temperament changes from joy to rage, from Standard English to Black English trying to make up a song:

"Walker. Ohhh! I ´ll stay here and rape your wife…as I so often used to do…as I so often used…" (59).

Thus, music becomes another means of communication, and it can be substituted for the spoken language that fails to fulfill its function between the characters.

5.2.5 Narrative devices in the play

The Slave is described as ´A Fable in a Prologue and two Acts´. Baraka intends to begin the narration of his play by a prologue that introduces the central character, Walker Vessels. The speaker of the prologue appears as an old, white-haired field slave dressed in ragged clothing, delivering his long monologue. In fact, the playwright chooses to use a prologue to lead the audience from their world into the world of the play establishing the setting, the themes as well as some details about the play.

As previously stated, *The Slave* deals with racial conflict in The United States. Baraka presents Walker as a leader of a violent radical black liberation movement whose aim is to kill the white society. This raging battle against the whites occurs, however, at some indeterminate moment in the future. So, the play is timeless on the subject of race conflict.

As far as the setting of the play is concerned, it takes place in the Easleys' living room, where Walker holds a gun after entering the house of his ex-white wife Grace. Furthermore, *The Slave* is presented from the third-person point of view asserting the narrator's omniscience. In other words, the narrator knows all the thoughts and emotions of all the characters in the play which allows the audience to see into the mind of each character. Using third person omniscient allows also various interpretations to the play associated with the plot. This latter is, par excellence, a ritual journey for the Black militant Walker Vessels, who is transmitted back to the old field slave bringing the plot of the play to a circular ending.

Motivated by the Civil Rights epoch of the late 1950s and early 1960s, Baraka wrote a revolutionary theatre of ritual violence.

Violence is, actually a fundamental ritual instrument in Baraka's play *The Slave* that portrays the murder of a white couple in the name of Black liberation. In addition, Baraka adopts, with many artists of the Theatre Movement, the ritual because, according to Olga Barrios, "They thought rituals were more powerful than *talking heads*. They believed that Western theatre was mainly talking in a drawing room, which life was taking place outside" (Olga Barrios).

Easley names, indeed, the rebellion Walker is leading a ´ritual drama´ represented in the repetition of the actions in the play. Moreover, Shelby Steele states:" Ritual in the new Black Theater is achieved through the repetition of patterns, symbols and values from drama to drama rather than the traditional religious method of repeating a single ceremony until it becomes ritual "(Steele 33).

With its stilted as well as its direct and structured speech, *The Slave* fulfills its function as a fable containing a moral. A part of this moral is, present in "the bifurcated personality of its Willie Best figure, the composite of slave and rebel" (Benston 183).

In fact, Walker, the rebel leader, has to step back into history in order to get rid of the psychic weight of white culture from his past. He must, therefore, leave Grace who is, indeed, a part of his past:

> "Grace. I guess that´s the point, now. Is that the point, Walker?
> Me being alone…as you have been now for so long? I´ll be that´s
> the point, huh? I´ll bet you came here to do exactly what you
> did…kill Brad, then take the kids, and leave me alone…to
> suffocate in the stink of my memories…Just like I did to you. I´m
> sure that´s the point. Right? (…)
>
> Walker. Yeah, Grace that´s the point. For sure, that´s the point" (Jones
> 83-84).

Besides, the playwright could not ignore the reference to music in the narration of the play. In other words, by incorporating the rhythmus of Blues music in *The Slave*, Baraka employs a fundamental element to African American culture that conveys a painful experience of black people. The old field slave ends his monologue in the prologue of the play singing Blues:

> "Walker. Or old, old bleus people moaning in their sleep,
> singing, man, oh, nigger, nigger, you still here, as hard as nails,

77

and takin´ no shit from nobody. He say, yeah, yeah, he say yeah,
yeah. He say, yeah, yeah, …goin´down slow, man. Goin´down
slow. He say…yeah, heh…"(45).

In short, Baraka as one of black writers who attempts to address the issue of race
with his writings adopts narrative devices that notify changing to the Civil Rights
Movement in The United States.

5.2.6 A comparison between *Dutchman* and *The Slave*

LeRoi Jones clarifies in his social essays: *Home*, the fundamental goal of the
revolutionary theatre that "should force change, it should be change" (Jones, *Home*
210).

Black playwrights succeeded, actually, in infusing new forms and new points of
view to the black theatre, intensifying their massage to achieve political change.
From the perspective of black theatre, Baraka´s two plays *Dutchman* and *The Slave*
are certainly examples of the Black Revolutionary Theatre. The two plays, published
together as one book, depict Black protagonists discovering themselves through their
confrontations with white society offering, however, variation in character and theme.

The black dramatist LeRoi Jones ends his plays with dead bodies´ scenes
employing the knife´s weapon and explosions that demonstrate the victory over the
enemy. Yet, each play has its own distinctive character that chooses his fate as a
means of liberation from the oppressor. While the black protagonist, Clay Williams,
loses his racial conflict in *Dutchman*, the black leader, Walker Vessels, wins the
revolution against the whites in *The Slave*.

In other words, LeRoi Jones presents his black protagonists in the two plays opposed
in point of view. The black loser in *Dutchman* chooses to stay in his insanity
following white models. He has actually two alternatives. Either to deny his

blackness and to live admiring the white´s world or he can rebel and murder asserting, therefore, his blackness and identity. The black Clay avoids the notion of revolution and he allows the white Lula to impose her values on him. Differently from Clay, Walker prepares already at the beginning of the play his revolutionary action. He appears ready to any lengths to fight for his cause. As a leader of an armed Black liberation movement, Walker is determined to be a revolutionary hero coming back to face his past represented by his former white wife, Grace, and the white intellectual Easley. This latter states that Walker´s revolution is an ´ugly idea´. Even though, Walker will continue on the path he has chosen.

In choosing insanity, Clay affirms his betrayal to the racial revolution. However, it is worthy pointing out that Clay is a rebel for he refuses to be influenced and criticized by the white society represented by Lula. Furthermore, the audience has sympathy for Clay because of his eventual powerless murder, whereas Walker does gain only disdain and hate from the audience that sees the Easleys as miserable victims of the revolutionary rage. Indeed, Jones portrays Grace and Easley´ fear and helplessness humanizing the symbolic enemy (Kaufman 200).

A detailed study of the two plays would not reveal only reversed parallels in character, but it indicates variance in the level of exploring the themes of the plays.

As previously mentioned, *Dutchman* is about hatred. The Slave takes, however, that theme to a whole different level. It is brutal and fierce depicting the white liberal couple dying in an explosion that destroys their home. As a matter of fact, Jones determines in The Slave on Attacking and Accusing applying the concept of the Revolutionary Theatre that "must Accuse and Attack anything that can be accused and attacked. It must Accuse and Attack because it is a theatre of victims" (Jones 211).

On the contrary, *Dutchman* is retrained in its form that reports anger. Jones in *Dutchman* is "still probing and the result is the tension that allows art. But in the

Attacking and Accusing of *The Slave*, tension is relaxed, form is gone; and propaganda, the Revolutionary Theatre; takes over" (Black as victim).

So, *Dutchman* states hatred and predicts the race revolution that later occurs in *The Slave*. Moreover, both of the plays explore the theme of search and the theme of sanity. It is well to remind ourselves that *Dutchman* was written in Jones' transitional epoch, in which he himself was in search for an orientation in the American society. He depicts the white Lula eating an apple, and tempting men she meet by arguing that they help her search in her own way. She tells Clay: "Lula. I even got into this train, going some other way than mine. Walked down the aisle…searching you out "(Jones 7).

Baraka's protagonist, Clay, searches also for himself by playing the role of assimilation, admiring the white world. He requires an awareness of his position in a society that does not allow him to be part of it. In their racial and verbal confrontation, *Dutchman's* characters test their sanities throughout their behavior to each other. The Bohemian Lula fluctuates between moments of sanity and flashbacks that provide the audience an insight into her past. She lives in an imaginary world aiming to draw Clay in to it. Clay, however, stands up after being provoked by Lula mocking his imitation of whites. In response, the Black Clay starts voicing Black Nationalist beliefs asserting his sanity and power:

"Clay. If I'm a middle –class fake white man…let me be. And let me be in the way I want" (34).

Clay knows, at this moment, that it is sane to acknowledge his blackness arguing that the blacks are actually sane expecting their victory:

"Clay. My people. They don't need me to claim them. They got legs and arms of their own…They don't need all these words. They don't need any defense…They' ll murder you, and have very rational explanations "(35).

Jones discusses again in *The Slave* the themes of search and sanity, but in an apparent way. According to Lindberg, "The race war is now open...The roles are now actual, not symbolic" (Lindberg 145).

Indeed, the central character of *The Slave*, Walker Vessel, introduces the play in a prologue that attacks the whole nature of society blaming history of turning people into killers and liars. In the play, the leader Walker makes up his mind to desert the battle field, and to return to his past represented by his former white wife and his two mulatto daughters. In essence, coming back to the home of his former masters, is serving his ties with his past, which Walker himself considers as an insane part of his life. In his insane life, he valued personal ideas that he had to relinquish for the sake of revolution. Grace, however, could not understand Walker´s militant revolution. She screams many times in horror: "You´re an insane man" affirming that Walker is out of his mind. He then replies"...being out of your mind is the only thing that qualifies you stay alive...Easley was in his right mind...That´s the reason he´s dead" (Jones 82).

This dialogue repeats the cross-accusations between Lula and Clay "with the difference that Walker has consciously passed into the historic personality that Clay foretold for his people" (Lindberg 146).

At the end of *The Slave*, Walker appears triumphant: More explosions are heard, the white couple is dead and Walker reveals that his two mulatto daughters are dead too. In effect, Walker comes back and kills his daughters, sacrificing his past loves, to rescue them from living as the whites. Jones reverses in his two plays *Dutchman* and *The Slave*, the roles of his two protagonists Walker and Clay. This latter plays a white role that costs him his life.

On the other hand, both of the plays have circular ending, signifying apparently that no change has occurred. Baraka ends *Dutchman* depicting Lula biting into an apple, an exact repetition of the beginning of the play. Likewise, *The Slave* concludes with Walker who is awakened by the faint cries of a child, and he is then transmuted back to the old field that appeared in the prologue. The violent and circular ending of the two plays allows, in fact, no hope for a solution to the race conflict.

In spite of the fact that Baraka´s plays *Dutchman* and *The Slave* offer many striking parallels and reversals, they confirm the sense that they are connected with each other sharing the issue of racial revolution.

6 Conclusion

The issue of equal rights presented an essential challenge to America. Although the Civil War did bring an official end to slavery in the United States signaling the start of the Reconstruction, all blacks in the South were disenfranchised, excluded from voting rights and all public facilities. In fact, all kinds of segregation were completely legitimized through the Supreme Court´s ruling in the *Plessy vs. Ferguson* case 1896 that required the doctrine of "separate but equal". The African Americans had to wait until 1954 to overturn this ruling when the Supreme Court in Brown vs. the Board of Education declared racial segregation in public schools unconstitutional. Furthermore, more protests continued demanding equal rights. The Montgomery bus boycott was, indeed, one of the greatest victories of the Civil Rights Movement when Rosa Parks was arrested and charged with violating the bus segregation law, because she refused to give up her seat for a white man on a Montgomery bus. The struggle between segregationists and integrationists intensified when "The Little Rock Nine" enrolled at Central High School in Little Rock, Arkansas. The protest ended allowing integration in Little Rock.

Several African American leaders and lawyers kept fighting and pushed the struggle for racial equality forward. Throughout the world the name of Martin Luther King, Jr. and Malcolm X are met with recognition and respect. Both of them, despite their differences, made the struggles of African-Americans an international issue. In other words, the two great African American leaders fought in words- for a single goal- freedom and equality for African Americans. Nonviolence and civil resistance were prominent strategies of the legendary civil rights activist Dr. Martin Luther King Jr. His dream has eventually changed the world. On the other hand, Malcolm X was a Muslim minister who believed that all people, regardless of race, are equal.

Several revolutionary writers chose to rebel with their literary works, reflecting the black man´s vision of the white society. In this respect, this book chose to study the biography of the black dramatist Amiri Baraka, portraying his former life as LeRoi Jones and his life as a black revolutionary politician. As a black dramatist and a founder of the Black Arts Repertory Theatre, it was worthy to examine Jones' dramatic credo, called "The Revolutionary Theatre". In essence, our choice of analyzing Jones´ two plays *Dutchman* and *The Slave* is deliberate, for they belong to The Revolutionary Theatre that threatens the white oppressor and calls for revolution and violence. Throughout the two plays, Baraka explores a number of race themes presenting the two plays timeless on the subject of the race conflict. The two plays depict, in fact, the tragic contradictions of its central characters asserting their victimization. Both of the protagonists remain victims mainly of their philosophy.

On the other hand, what Baraka was fighting against through his literary art is still prevalent in The United States today. In effect, demonstrations against racism and police violence have been recently organized across the United States and around the world, demanding justice for Michael Brown, an 18-year-old unarmed African American who was shot multiple times and killed by a police officer in the past few months in Ferguson. Furthermore, the black community is outraged at the non-indictment of the Ferguson Police Officer, which affirms that the fight for civil rights hasn't been won yet. Indeed, thousands of demonstrators scheduled to rally against the police brutality that is linked to racism, with the hope of reviving the fight for civil rights.

Amiri Baraka stressed, about five decades ago, in his famous social essays, *Home*: "But the fact that Negroes in America are still field slaves or house slaves, the mode of oppression depending on the accident of social breeding, one group having easy chairs in its cells" (Jones, *Home* 138).

Baraka has been, nevertheless, criticized by many who hold the view that his shocking plays *Dutchman* and *The Slave* are far from underpinning racial consciousness. We think that the rage expressed in the two plays may be justified, but the action is unacceptable. With no doubt, Baraka´s plays left an impact on the world. We applaud the black dramatist Baraka for writing about the issue of race in his time, and we wish to see *Dutchman* and *The Slave* performed on stage.

Works Cited

Baraka, Amiri. *The Autobiography of LeRoi Jones*. New York: Freundlich Books, 1984.

--. *Raise, Race, Rays, Raze: Essays Since 1965*. New York: Random House, 1971.

Barrios, Olga."Amiri Baraka: The Ritual of History and The Self in The Slave"<**Error! Hyperlink reference not valid.**> 30.Oct.2014

Bennett, Jr., Lerone. *What Manner of Man: A memorial Biography of Martin Luther King, Jr.* New York: Pocket Books, 1968.

Benston, Kimberly W. *Baraka: The Renegade and the Mask*. New Haven and London: Yale University Press, 1976.

Bracey,Jr. John H, and Harley, Sharon. "The Black Power Movement Part 1: Amiri Baraka from Black Arts to Black Radicalism" <ttp://www.lexisnexis.com/documents/academic/upa_cis/10721_blackpowermovempt1.pdf> 01.Nov.2014

"Brown at 60: The Doll Test".<http://www.naacpldf.org/brown-at-60-the-doll-test> 10.03.2014

"Brown v. Board of Education".<http://www.watson.org/~lisa/blackhistory/early-civilrights/brown.html >12.03.2014

Costello, Donald.P. "LeRoi Jones: Black Man as Victim" <http://www.nathanielturner.com/leroijones2.htm> 02.Dec.2014

Darby, Jean. *Martin Luther King, Jr.* Minneapolis: Lerner Publishing Group, 1990. "Davis v. School Board of Prince Edward County (Virginia)". <http://www.civilrights.org/education/brown/davis.html> 15.03.2014

Dierenfield, Bruce J. *The Civil Rights Movement*. Harlow: Pearson Longman, 2008.

Effiong, Philip Uko. "Amiri Baraka's Revolutionary Theatre: A Reapplication of African Ritual Paradigms". < http://www.philip-effiong.com/Baraka-Revolutionary-Theatre.pdf> 27.Oct.2014

---. *In Search of a Model for African- American Drama: A Study of Selected Plays by Lorraine Hansberry, Amiri Baraka, and Ntozake Shange*. Lanham: UP of America, 2000.

Essien-Udom, Essien Udosen. *Black Nationalism: The Rise of The Black Muslims in The U.S.A.* Harmondsworth: Penguin Books, 1962.

Freyer, Tony A. *Little Rock on Trial. Cooper v. Aaron and School Desegregation*. Lawrence: UP of Kansas, 2007.

"History". < http://wwwbbc.co.uk/history/people/martin_luther_king.shtml>30.Sep.2014 Hornby, Albert Sidney. *Oxford Advanced Learner´s Dictionary of Current English*. Oxford: Oxford UP, 1974.

Hudson,Theodore R. *From LeRoi Jones to Amiri Baraka: The Literary Works*. Durhman: Duke University Press, 1972.

Jones, LeRoi. *Dutchman and The Slave*. New York: Morrow Quill Paperbacks, 1964.

---. *Home: Social Essays*. New York: William Morrow & Co., INC, 1966.

Kaufman, Micheal W. "The delicate World of Reprobation: A Note on the Black Revolutionary Theater". *The Theater of Black Americans: A collection of Critical Essays*. Eds.Errol Hill. Engelwood Cliffs. New Jersey: Prentice Hall, Inc., 1980.200.

Lacey, Henry C. *To Raise, Destroy, and Create: The Poetry, Drama, and Fiction of Imamu Amiri Baraka (LeRoi Jones)*. Troy, NY: Whitston Publishing, 1981.

"Letter from Birmingham Jail (King, Jr.)"<http://www.africa.upenn.edu/Articles_Gen/ Letter_Birmingham.html>02.Oct.2014

Lincoln, Charles Eric. *The Black Muslims in America. (Third Edition).* Michigan: Wm.B. Eerdmans Publishing Co, 1994.

Lindberg, John. "Dutchman and The Slave: Companions in Revolution". *Imamu Amiri Baraka(Leroi Jones) A Collection of Critical Essays.* Eds. Kimberly W. Benston. New York: Prentice-Hall, Inc., Engelwood Cliffs, 1978.145.

"Little Rock Crisis, 1957". < http://www.blackpast.org/aah/little-rock-crisis-1957> 10.04.2014

Luther King, Jr. Martin. *Stride Toward Freedom: The Montgomery Story.* London: Gollancz, 1959.

Marable, Manning. *Malcolm X: A Life of Reinvention.* London: Penguin Books, 2011.

McCartney,Martha."Virginia'sFirstAfricans."<http://encyclopediavirginia.org/Virginia_s_First_Afr icans> 03.03.2014

"Metaphorical Representations for America and the Oppressed"   <Error! Hyperlink reference not valid.

"NAACP & the Ada Sipuel Case". < http://www.nathanielturner.com/adasipuelcase.htm>

06.03.2014

Parks, Rosa, Haskins, James. *My Story: Rosa Parks.* Dial Books, 1992.

Patterson, James T. *Brown v. Board of Education: A Civil Rights Milestone and Its Troubled Legacy.* Oxford: Oxford UP, 2001.

"Selma to Montgomery March (1965)" <http://mlk-kpp01.standford.edu/index.php/encyclopedia/enc_selma_to_montgomery_march/> 05.Oct.2014

Sollors, Werner. *Amiri Baraka/ Leroi Jones: The Quest for a "Populist Modernism"*. New
York: Columbia UP, 1978.

Steele, Shelby. "Notes on Ritual in the New Black Theater." *The Theater of Black Americans: A collection of Critical Essays.*Eds. Errol Hill. Engelwood Cliffs. New Jersey: Prentice Hall, Inc., 1980.

Stone, Judy. "If It´s Anger…Maybe That´s Good: An Interview with LeRoi Jones." *Conversations with Amiri Baraka*. Eds.Charlie Reilly. UP of Mississipi, 1994. 10.

Sunnemark, Fredrick. An Inescapable Network of Mutuality: Discursivity and Ideology in the Rhetoric of Martin Luther King, Jr. Göteborg: Acta Universitatis Gothoburgensis, 2001.

"Sweatt v. Painter". < http://en.wikipedia.org/wiki/Sweatt_v._Painter> 12.03.2014

"The Legend of the Flying Dutchman". < http://www.ghost-story.co.uk/index.php/ghost-stories/378-the-legend-of-the-flying- dutchman> 10.07.2014

"The Story behind the Bus". < http://www.thehenryford.org/exhibits/rosaparks/story.asp>
02.04.2014

Watts, Jerry Gafio. Amiri Baraka: The Politics and Art of a Black Intellectual. New York:
New York UP, 2001.

White, John. Martin Luther King, Jr., and the Civil Rights Movement in America. Hanley, Stoke-on-Trent: J.H. Brooks (Printers) Ltd, 1991.

Williams, Sherley Anne. "The Search for Identity in Baraka´s Dutchman." Imamu Amiri Baraka(Leroi Jones) A Collection of Critical Essays. Eds. Kimberly W. Benston. New York: Prentice-Hall, Inc., Engelwood Cliffs, 1978.136.

"World History Project"<http://worldhistoryproject.org/1964/2/the-nation-of-islam-makes-threats-against-malcolm-x> 10.Oct.2014

Wormser, Richard. "Jim Crow Stories: The Rise and Fall of Jim Crow". http://www.pbs.org/wnet/jimcrow/stories-events-gaines.html 05.03.2014

ya Salaam, Kalamu. "A Conversation with Amiri Baraka". <http://www.english.illinois.edu/maps/poets/a_f/baraka/salaam.htm> 15.Oct.2014

---. "Historical Overviews of The Black Arts Movement". <http://www.english.illinois.edu/maps/blackarts/historical.htm> 15.Oct.2014

Biographies

Naoual Kamal is a researcher at University of Mainz, Faculty of Translation Studies, Linguistics and Cultural Studies, Germany. She holds a Graduate Diploma Translator from Johannes Gutenberg University of Mainz, Faculty of Translation Studies, Linguistics and Cultural Studies in Germersheim, Germany. She earned a Certificate of German Language for University entrance from Studienkolleg in Halle(Saale), Germany. She obtained a Certificate Central Mittelstufenprüfung from Goethe Institut in Casablanca, Morocco. She holds a Bachelor of Arts in English language and Literature from Chouaib Doukkali University Faculty of Letters and Human Sciences in Eljadida, Morocco. Her areas of interests are: Translation Studies, Translation, Cultural Studies, Intercultural Communication, Linguistics and Literature.

Karima Bouziane is an Assistant Professor and researcher at National School of Commerce and Management, Chouaib Doukkali University. She holds a Doctorate degree in Translation Studies and Intercultural Communication from LERIC, Chouaib Doukkali University, El Jadida, Morocco. She also holds a Master's Degree in Cross-cultural Communication and Translation Studies from the Department of English of the same university. Her areas of interest are: English for Specific Purposes, Translation Studies Research, Translation and Globalization, Localization, Translation and Cognition, Advertising, Neuromarketing, Intercultural Business Communication, Linguistics, Literature, Gender Studies, Semiotics, Art (painting) exhibitions. She is author of the book: *Cultural Transfer in the Translation of Advertising from English into Arabic.*